MY STORY *God's Glory*

Authentic Stories of Victorious Journeys Beyond Pain and Into Purpose

MANAGING EDITOR
Timeko Whitaker

Authentic Identity Coaching

PUBLISHED BY
Authentic Identity Coaching, LLC
P.O. Box 36131
Indianapolis, IN 46236

www.authenticinstitute.com
(317) 710-9533

Please contact
Authentic Identity Coaching
for quantity discounts

©2016 Timeko Whitaker

ISBN: 978-0-9863401-1-6
Library of Congress Control Number: 2016908440
Printed in the United States of America

Book Layout by Vision Communications
Cover Design by Studio 5 Agency
General Editing by Dee Dee Cooper
Photography by Beyond The Focus Photography
Photography by Lor-El Vision Photography

TABLE OF CONTENTS

ABOUT THE MANAGING EDITOR

Timeko L. Whitaker, Founder and CEO of Authentic Identity Coaching, LLC is the wife of Eric Whitaker and the mother of Daelin and Eyuana Whitaker. She is a gifted Life Coach and International Speaker who challenges all to live an authentic life on purpose.

Timeko holds a Bachelor's Degree in Human Resource Management and a Master's Degree in Theology.

Timeko is a certified Human Behavior Consultant (specializing in DISC) and a certified Life Coach through Christian Coach Institute. Her coaching sessions are life changing and impact attendees of all demographical backgrounds while her "5D Authentically Me" empowerment seminars continue to empower clients both locally and internationally.

Timeko is a certified John Maxwell Team Member, Speaker, Trainer and Coach equipped to develop and train worldwide leaders. Timeko is a published author of "Hidden Identity-Untold Stories of Pastor's Wives" and a contributing author of "The Power of Mentorship" with Zig Ziglar, Brian Tracy and other amazing authors. Timeko is also the Managing Editor/Publisher of "A Piece of Me – My Journey of Authenticity."

Timeko enjoys spending time as a part-time host

on TBN's WCLJ-TV's "Joy In Our Town" where she interviews community leaders, businesses and organizations that make a difference in our society.

In 2015 Timeko and her husband Eric launched Authentic Identity Institute, where they train and certify 5D Identity Coaches and Human Behavior Consultants. Timeko's goal is to help everyone she encounters embrace their authenticity and significance. Through speaking, training and coaching she motivates all to reach higher heights, embrace values and achieve their dreams.

With over twenty years of military service, culminating in her retirement in 2008, coupled with ten years of Pastoral service; Timeko has committed her life to serving God through serving others and has dedicated her business to helping all discover the power of authenticity.

Authentic Identity Coaching, LLC
P.O. Box 36131
Indianapolis, IN 46236
(317) 710-9533
authenticidentity@gmail.com
www.authenticinstitute.com
www.johnmaxwellgroup.com/timekowhitaker

Introduction

1 Peter 5:10, *And the God of all grace, who called you to his eternal glory in Christ, after you have suffered a little while, will himself restore you and make you strong, firm and steadfast.*

As a Certified Christian Life Coach, there's nothing more fulfilling than witnessing the authentic journey of one who strives to move past every block and barrier to pursue and embrace the call upon their lives. Daily, I encounter amazing people with untold stories that if fully revealed would send shockwaves through the very heart of any reader, yet they continue their relentless walk of faith. Each of these authors have partnered with Authentic Identity Coaching and allowed us to play a small part in the BIG that God is doing in their lives. These strong, bold and courageous women have all embraced the idea that they are to be good stewards over not only their time, talents and treasures but also over their testimonies. They've come to a realization that the significance of their past can aid in bringing others out of a place of pain and into a place of permission... Permission to move forward, permission to forgive, permission to allow God's glory to be revealed through their story.

Our hope is that each chapter and testimony will ignite something deep on the inside of you that will give you strength and courage to maneuver past obstacles and to advance in life. We pray the words will emanate from the pages to bring life to every dead situation you may be facing. We pray to bring hope and reassurance that your life has only just begun and as you move forward in faith, you'll embrace the truth that the best is yet to come. Journey with us as we give God all the glory.

MANAGING EDITOR

Timeko Whitaker

MY STORY *God's Glory*

Authentic Stories of Victorious Journeys Beyond Pain and Into Purpose

Tonya Kinchelow

Tonya Kinchelow wears many hats - wife, mother, career woman, community leader, mentor, and now, published author.

She has pursued her dreams and succeeded at each of them. Born and raised in Indianapolis, IN, she attended Arlington High School. Tonya married her 8th grade sweetheart, Jeffery, in 1989. They were blessed with a daughter, Ayana.

Tonya started her first entrepreneurial adventure in 1994 when she opened her own beauty salon. As a cosmetologist, she freelanced as a make-up artist for Mac Cosmetics and Nordstrom's. She traveled for 25 years competing and training in the beauty industry. Upon retiring from her first career, she quickly pursued her passion for real estate. She is now a real estate broker and the CEO of TK Realty Group at Keller Williams Realty. She is a leader in her community serving on several committees and boards.

Discovering her gift of encouragement, she mentors through Trusted Mentors and volunteers with Dress for Success. Tonya's passion is to serve. Those who know her will tell you that her true passion is found shopping for shoes, reading, traveling and finding new ways to renew her spirit.

CHAPTER ONE

God's Grace is Truly Amazing

FROM SISTER FRIEND TO MOTHER

Sometimes in life we have relationships that lose their focus and become less than what they were meant to be. My childhood, teen years and adulthood was molded by this type of relationship.

Hey girl!

Hey girl! How you doin?

I'm fine... How you doin?

I'm ok, my chest has been hurting.

You need to see about that.

I know... I'm going to call my doctor tomorrow.

"Hey Girl!" is how my mother and I talk to one another. This is typical of our conversations. "Hey Girl. Where are you?" or "Hey Girl! Meet me here." or "Hey Girl! Meet me there." No matter what we were talking about, it started with a "Hey Girl!" Mom was like a sister to me, a friend. It was not the traditional mother/daughter relationship. It was my grandmother, who was the matriarch of the family that we all considered mama over all. Grandmother was the boss.

Looking back maybe that is why my mother and I had such a rocky relationship growing up. We were always back and forth, up and down... always drama! Just like siblings. One day during an argument the relationship was broken and we did not speak to one another for a year. This was my mother and though we were in the same city, we never spoke or saw each other nor did we make an effort to fix the mess. I quietly kept tabs on her by talking with her best friend, Lee Ann.

I wasn't aware how deeply the break in our relationship affected me, until my mother reached out to me through a letter. There it was in my mailbox, a thick envelope with no return address. I opened it. It was a letter from my mother. I was shocked, stunned, happy and nervous all at once. I opened the envelope with hesitation. I paused before I began to read it. My mind was flooding with thoughts of our past relationship struggles. My apprehension was that by reading this letter I could be sent on a not buckled up roller coaster ride, which made me ask myself if I was really ready to go back into the tricks and games of the enemy. For a brief moment I almost let what used to be cause me to miss something great.

It took me several times to read the letter because I cried so hard the first few times. When I finally made it through, it brought sunshine to my soul, my spirit and my being. We met soon after and talked from the heart for probably the first time in our entire relationship. We decided to let the past be the past, learn from it and move forward to a new beginning. During the time we were apart my mom became an evangelist. She's always been in church, but she was noticeably different. She had wholeheartedly given her life to Christ. It was a shock to me! My mother? Wow! She talked, walked, prayed and mentored. She inspired me and we had a blast. We hung out at church events, shopped and prayed. She was a super grandma to my daughter. It was God's amazing grace!

I finally had my mother and it was wonderful! The time we shared was indescribable. It was like heaven had opened up. I was learning so much from her. The way she said "I love you" was like a heated blanket on a cold winter's night. Her words of wisdom were so soothing and encouraging. She poured into me for 5 years a lifetime of love. Things changed suddenly. "Hey Girl" went to the doctor and was diagnosed with colon cancer which later moved to her brain, then to her lymph nodes. Jesus, Mary and Joseph! It was as though someone was squeezing my neck and my eyes were popping out of the sockets. Breathless and stunned, I wondered how this could be happening! Within 6 months she went on to be with the Lord with a smile on her face. I felt like someone was holding me under water and I couldn't breathe. Why? Why? Why would God let it happen this way? Why would He give her to me, saved and full of life then take her away? I asked so many questions and I wanted answers. In a small still voice I heard the Lord speak to me and say "she was mine; she was only loaned to you." I had the honor of serving her and being with her until she drew her last breath. That, too, was God's amazing grace!

My heart was broken and I was devastated. Through my faith in God, the healing began and I could smile again. It had been a few months since I really smiled and it felt good. I could feel the heaviness begin to lift off of my heart.

On the brink of healing from the loss of my mother, the phone rang one morning at 8 a.m. My grandmother, Mrs. Dorothy, had fallen and was rushed to the hospital. My husband and I jetted to the hospital. My grandmother, my rock, my heart, my friend, my world, and my safe place was gone. Just like that she had passed away. Lord! Lord! Lord!! I yelled! I was an emotional wreck! I was mad, lost, hurt, scared and stunned. The devil had a chokehold on me. I thought there was a curse on me. I thought it was something I did that caused my two anchors to be gone. It was like an elephant was standing on my chest. I felt I couldn't go on without them. The day of the funeral I stood over her and cried. My cry was not a "shoulda woulda coulda" cry. It was simply that I loved her and I was going to miss her! She had given me everything I could ask for. She made everything right. Her voice was my safe place. It took a while before I can say I truly recovered from the loss. Yet God kept me because I had a praying grandmother and because He loves me. God's amazing grace once again was shown to me.

THE BAIT OF SATAN

The loss of my grandmother and mother crippled me. I felt like I was breathing through a stirrup straw gasping for life. As the months passed by I could see daylight again; I was able to breathe again. It finally felt like I was on solid ground and could begin moving forward. Not so…

I went back to work after being off for a few months. Three days after being back to work, I answered my phone to hear a voice saying, "Your husband is my daughter's father." Jesus! My Lord! My Lord! She continued talking. I wanted to hang up but her words captivated me. She was telling me my husband (the man I've been with since I was 13 years old) had committed adultery with her 11 years prior and they had a child together. Those words hit me like a ton of bricks. My only thought was, "The devil's trying to kill me." I felt like an 18 wheeler Mack truck had run over me, backed up and ran over me again. We hung up. I immediately called my husband who denied it to the fullest. I don't know what I was feeling at that moment. I was emotionally frozen. I managed to get through the day and went to my friend Cathy's house. I cried so hard I thought my insides were going to come out of my mouth. I was hurt and I believe all the hurt I had experienced within the last months and years came out with that cry. As I was crying I heard my friend crying just as hard as I was. I found myself consoling her. She held me and we cried together. What a friend! God's amazing grace in the form of friendship.

We later found out it was true. I was so hurt. Believe me when I say it was H-E-double hockey sticks in our home. This was a devastating blow to my mind, spirit and soul. It really tore a hole in my heart. I felt barren, lost, confused, angry, crushed and hollow inside. The road to recovery and restoration was a long, grueling, painstaking process. To look at him set all my organs ablaze. There were times I didn't want to pray at all, let alone pray for him. I am thankful for my cousin, Shelly who became our Intercessor. She interceded on our behalf and God listened.

Surrounded by prayer warriors, friends, our pastor and lay pastors my husband fought with all that was in him to save our marriage. The pain I was feeling was deep. I was not sure I would recover from this one. My heart felt the loss of everything that was dear to me. All that I trusted had either died or betrayed me. I couldn't pray because I didn't know what to say to God. Countless days and nights, my dearest friend Sharon prayed with me. God used her to teach me how to forgive my husband, lay hands on him and myself, what it meant to lay flat before the Lord, the blood of the lamb, letting

His Spirit permeate my very essence and so much more. My grandmother, Mrs. Dorothy planted the seed and God used Sharon to water it and birth the prayer warrior in me to release the power that healed my marriage. Another obstacle overcome by God's amazing grace to me.

WHAT DOESN'T KILL YOU...

Two months later I went in for my annual exam. My husband and I... (Yeah I'm a big baby when it comes to doctors so he's always gone with me). During the exam my doctor found some cysts on my ovaries. He suggested they be removed. The following month I went in to have a simple outpatient procedure to remove the cysts. The procedure would take about two hours and I would be off work for a couple of days. About twenty minutes into the procedure, the doctor found three more cysts. They were larger - the size of a silver dollar, a golf ball and a grapefruit. The doctor leaves me on the operating table still sedated to tell my husband the cyst's are very large, may burst and could cause major damage. He explained to my husband how the surgery would prevent us from having more children and needed his permission to proceed. This really threw him for a loop because this was to be a simple outpatient procedure. Now to hear we couldn't have more children and not be able to discuss it with me put him between a rock and a hard place. We didn't plan on having any more children since our daughter was already eighteen years old. But to have our right of choice taken away from us was something different. The burden of this decision rested solely on my husband's shoulders. He decided proceeding with the surgery was the best option. The next hurdle he had to face was telling me. When my doctor and husband told me, I have to tell you I was numb and for some reason I wanted to give up on life. Where was God's grace now?

What is going on? Is there a curse on me? No way should one person have to go through this. Why does it have to be me? I was off work for four months. We were not prepared for me to be off work for this extended period of time. This time was very challenging. It was during the time my daughter was graduating from high school and going to the prom amongst other things. Lord, how am I going to help her? This is one of the most important times of her life. She needs me and I'm bedridden for the next three months. For days I lay in my dark bedroom with my comforter up to my eye lids. All I wanted to do was stay in my dark room. I had no appetite; I was weak and I had no desire to do anything. As I lay there watching Oprah interview Whitney Houston, she sang a song from her CD. As she sang, my skin slowly pulled back from my bones. It was like a ray of light beamed on me. "I didn't know my own strength" was the song that ministered to my heart and to my spirit. I thought I'd never make it through, I thought I would break. I got through all the pain. I was not built to break! Everything I needed was inside of me. I crashed down and I tumbled but I did not crumble. I didn't know my own strength. It was like my heavenly father said to me "you were not built to break." I got up after many many tears and ran straight to Target and bought the CD and played it several times and I do mean several times a day.

God's amazing grace was there all the time; we made it happen for our daughter. Stitches and all, I was able to be at her graduation. She had a very blessed senior year with prom and graduation. She didn't miss a beat and neither did I. That was the beginning of my healing process. The words to that song and Isaiah 40:31 "...they that wait upon the Lord shall renew their strength; they shall mount up with wings as eagles..." helped me heal and not just heal but heal without scars.

NUGGETS IN MY BUCKET...

My cup runneth over as I look to my God daily for His guidance, protection and direction. He just keeps blessing me, taking care of me and protecting me; He keeps saving me and showing me grace and mercy. As I write my story, I realize how awesome it is that God has healed me without scars. My husband and I are doing great and we have so much fun together. We've been married 27 years and we are still in love. It seems things are even better now than before. We've been through a lot together and God just keeps lifting us higher and higher. Nothing's too dirty for God to make worthy. What the devil meant for bad my God turned around for my good. I have a daughter that words alone cannot express how much and what she means to me. We have a relationship that is precious to me. She has been my biggest supporter, cheerleader and breath of fresh air. Her love is empowering and refreshing. She's priceless.

> *Nothing's too dirty for God to make worthy.*

My life has become an awesome, great and wonderful testimony of His Amazing Grace. I have been blessed to have people in my life that mean the world to me. My Uncle Milton is one of those people and the smartest man I know. No matter how dim it may look, he always finds a way to make the sun shine on my situation. I have a career that I love! I've met so many great people that have become clients as well as friends. I haven't mentioned my dad, but God has given me beauty for ashes with that relationship. We were estranged for many years, but now, we are like two peas in a pod. We travel, read, eat and pray together. My dad not only stepped up to the plate, he's batting it out the park. I have siblings that I love to spend time with

Another one of my dearest friends, Tracey, said to me... "Sis, you should write a book." "Girl please!" I said, yet here I am 7 years later writing My Story for God's Glory. I never thought I would be opening my treasure trove and sharing my gems with the world. I'm a firm believer that you have to watch what is spoken over your life and watch what you allow in your spirit. God 's word tells us in Psalm 23:4 that when you are going through a storm, remember you're going through, you're not staying there. You have to have people who encourage you. I was given double for my trouble when God so graciously gave me a stabilizer in my friend, Penny. She keeps me grounded in God's word and reminds me that everyone has a story and that everybody can't sit on the front row of your life. Some people are supposed to be in the nose bleed section.

I love the poem Footprints, "It was then that I carried you." I know God carried me when there were only two footprints in the sand. I know He favored me and I know He loves me. He just keeps blessing me. God's blood still has miraculous power! When you see broken, God sees Beautiful. He will help you believe and He will restore you piece by piece. He will heal you without scars. 1st Peter 5:7 says " ...*Casting all your cares [all your anxieties, all your worries, and all your concerns, once and for all] on Him, for He cares about you [with deepest affection, and watches over you very carefully]*" (Amplified) God truly cares for you. Whenever you're going through a storm God knows; He sees and He cares. Surround yourself with people who will pray for and with you. He is no respecter of persons and will do the same for you. Tap into His grace today!

My future is so bright I need sunglasses. God's grace is truly AMAZING!

Carmen Randolph

Carmen was born in Indianapolis, Indiana. She graduated from Warren Central High School. Carmen served six years in the United States Army as a combat medic.

She attended Ivy Tech Community College where she earned an Associate's of Science Degree. She later attended Indiana Wesleyan University where she earned a Bachelor's of Science Degree. Carmen currently attends Western Governor's University where She will complete a Master's Degree in Business Administration in January 2017. Carmen is a Registered Respiratory Therapist and a Registered Polysomnographic Technologist. She's a Sleep Lab Manager for Community Health Network where she manages the operations of six Sleep/Wake Disorders Centers within the network. Carmen is a certified 5D coach and DISC Trainer through AIC's Authentic Identity Institute. She has two beautiful children, Darius and Imani Randolph whom she is so proud of.

Carmen is the Founder/CEO of Create No Limits Coaching. She enjoys reading, gardening, and winemaking. She absolutely loves being on the beach and looking at the ocean. There is something so spiritual about the vastness of the water. It is too great to behold all at once and it reminds her of God's love. Carmen's mission is to empower people to push past their problems and pursue their purpose. Her ministry is focused on being a light to people in dark places and speaking love and hope back into their lives through Jesus Christ.

CHAPTER TWO

More Than A Conqueror

I've been through a lot of things in my life, as I'm sure most people have. I believe that dilemmas derail your destiny. Grab ahold of those things and denounce them. Break up the foundation on which your life is built. The lies told to you have to be exposed. The hurts, pains, and abuse have to be exposed. Expose all those skeletons and get down to the truth of the matter. Then you can redesign, restructure, and rebuild your life the way God intended it to be. It doesn't happen overnight but, it happens.

Jesus said, *"If you hold to my teaching, you are really my disciples. 32 Then you will know the truth, and the truth will set you free."* (John 8:31-32)

The Foundation

At a very early age I felt like I didn't belong here on Earth. I belonged nowhere. I was the youngest of my mom and dad's three kids. My skin tone was high yellow, accented with a plethora of dark brown freckles. I didn't much resemble anyone in my immediate family. Family members said I had features of my late grandma, Ruth Anne Murry. I never met her. She passed away when my dad was 12 years old. I never even saw a picture of her so I don't know if we looked alike or not. It would have been nice to make that connection, to feel like I came from something. My mom and dad had several photo albums filled with pictures of their younger years. There were pictures of friends, cousins, aunts, uncles and other people I didn't know. It was fun to look through the pictures and ask my mom and dad questions about them. There were pictures of us kids too. My brother had pictures when he was a baby learning how to walk. My sister had newborn pictures from the hospital and other pictures in her toddler stages. There were no pictures of me as a baby. My pictures began around the age of 2 years old. I would ask my mom why I never had pictures taken as a baby. I'm not sure I ever got an answer I could accept as truth. As I grew older, I asked other family members if they had baby pictures of me. No one could come up with a single picture. I concluded that something was wrong. Either I reminded my parents of something they wanted to forget or my mere existence was so insignificant that it did not warrant being remembered. This piece of foundation formed.

I remember going to school one day. I must have been in the 3rd or 4th grade or around the age of eight or nine. My mom gave me a piece of paper and told me to give it to my teacher. She told me that my last name changed from her last name, Russell, to my dad's last name, Murry. My mom and dad never married. I left the hospital with my mother's last name but my sister and brother left the hospital with my father's last name. My dad often told the same stories over and over again, about how he rushed my mom to the hospital when she was in labor with me. He had been drinking heavily that night and when the hospital staff asked him who he was while helping my mom get checked in, he said he was the baby of the daddy instead of the daddy of the baby. Telling that story tickled him so much. He would laugh hysterically every time he told the story like he was telling it for the first time. I would ask him why I was not given his name at the hospital if he was there. He said he didn't remember what happened; it didn't get changed. I wanted to believe him but that answer was just not believable since they had done this twice before me with my brother and sister. I concluded they didn't want me. Something happened, and they didn't want me. I felt like a stranger in that family, unloved, unwanted, and insignificant. This piece of foundation formed.

Thoughts of my childhood don't hold many pleas-ant memories. I'm sure it wasn't all bad but the memo-ries that stick out do not bring me joy, mostly just sad-ness and pain. I was molested by a family member around the age of 10. I really didn't fully understand what was happening but I knew it wasn't right. We didn't talk about the good touch and bad touch in our house. Initially, I was afraid to tell my mother because I thought she would be mad at me. I didn't like what was happening, but I didn't know what to do about it. One night I got enough courage to tell my parents what was happening. They listened as I talked and they stared at me. After I finished talking, my mom told me to go to bed. I remember feeling sick to my stomach because I didn't know what to expect. I didn't know if she would come back in the room and yell at me or hit me so I got into the bed and put the covers over my head. I felt even more violated. I wanted one of them to hug me. I wanted them to tell me they would protect me and it would never happen again. Unfortunately, I never heard those words, not that night or any night to follow. We never talked about it again. I'm assuming they must have talked with the person who violated me because he never tried to touch me again. I still had to see him because he was in our family. Every time I saw him I remembered every detail of his actions. As a child, I had to deal with the disgust, hurt, and pain alone. This piece of foundation formed.

The foundation was now built and life was off to a rocky start. Feelings of being unwanted, insignificant, unloved, and violated led me down a dark path. I adopted a new way of thinking to cope with things. Since I felt unwanted, I adopted the attitude that I needed nobody. It seemed like I didn't matter to anyone; I set out to make a name for myself to show them I am somebody and I matter. Since I felt unloved, I would be on a search to find somebody to love me. Anybody that thought they would violate me had another thing coming. I wasn't ever going to go through that again. I was on a mission. I wanted revenge. I'm not sure on who. I was just angry and wanted to let everybody who ever hurt me know just how angry I was.

By the time I was 10 years old I experienced alcohol, marijuana, and cigarettes. By age 13, I was using all three regularly. This was not out of the ordinary in my living environment. I was around it all day every day. It seemed to be the go to answer for the adult's issues. Smoking and drinking gave me the grown up feeling. It also made me feel like I fit in with the other kids that were doing it. When I was with my clique I felt significant, like I was part of something. When that feeling would go away, I would get money to get high again. It became a vicious cycle. Drinking, drugs, promiscuity, heartbreaks, lies, and uncertainties describe my teen years. I went to church. I was saved and baptized but I wasn't living like it. I partied hard and played hard. This went on throughout high school. I had a wonderful Pastor, Kenneth Sullivan Sr. He and his wife, Joyce, prayed for me a lot. They would come to my house, pick me up, take me out to lunch and talk about getting my life together. I would leave them feeling like I wanted to change but it was easy to fall back into my daily routine. They never gave up on me. They kept praying for me and loving me. I didn't feel worthy of their kindness towards me and I eventually left the church. I continued on in my mess. After a while, I was tired of it. Once I graduated from high school I felt it was time to do something new.

The Restructuring

I graduated from High School in the summer of 1993. I enlisted in the United States Army that November. By now, I was worn out and tired of my life and the monotony of it all. I felt like there had to be more to life than this. I had a boyfriend I had dated on and off throughout high school. We were good friends and had talked about marriage after high school. We were young and naïve and had no idea what it meant to be married. He got upset when I told him I was leaving for the Army. I told him that once I settled in I would send for him. We talked on the phone a lot and made plans for him to come visit me in Augusta, Georgia. He agreed to come, and I was so excited. The Lord had other plans though.

A week before he could come, someone murdered him. My world came to a crashing end. I flew back to Indianapolis for the funeral. It seemed so unreal that one day we were planning our future together and now I was going to his funeral. I felt like he was the only person who wanted me and cared about me. Now he was gone; I felt so alone. I hated Indianapolis. It had so many bad memories for me - now this. I remember thinking, as I flew back to Georgia after the funeral, I would never come back to Indianapolis again. I felt hurt, numb, and depressed. When I got back to the military base I could not work. I shared my pain with a fellow soldier and told her I wanted to end my life. She then told one of our Sergeants and they had me placed under suicide watch on the Psychiatric Unit of the military hospital. I don't think I ever cried so hard and so long in my entire life. I felt like I had hit rock bottom. No matter how hard I tried, things just did not seem to work out for me. I didn't fit in anywhere. I had nobody to talk to that I felt really understood me. I wanted to die. I had no reason to live. I prayed for God to let me die. There was no relief for me, only torturous feelings.

The Rebuilding

God was ordering my steps all throughout my journey and I didn't realize it. I left Indianapolis for a reason. All the tragedies in my life happened for a reason. I stayed in the psychiatric unit of the Army Hospital for about a week. I prayed and cried and cried and prayed for a good part of that week. I prayed to God with my whole heart to help me get my life back together. He heard me and gave me another chance. When I left the hospital, the Lord allowed me to

> *God was ordering my steps all throughout my journey and I didn't realize it.*

see He ordered my steps and led me to Augusta, Georgia to save my life. Going to the Army was not something I had ever planned to do. It happened. It took a lot of crying, praying, seeking, and waiting on the Lord. He came through for me. He healed my brokenness - brokenness from feeling unwanted when I was a child; the feelings of insignificance; the feelings of being unloved; the scars of being violated; the loneliness from losing my best friend. He took the heaviness of it all away. Yes, it still hurt me but I felt like I wanted to start over in spite of all that stuff and live again. It was an unexplainable joy that made me want to scream a sigh of relief.

I eventually got back on my feet and worked towards getting my life together. In time He blessed me to experience marriage, motherhood, a great education, and a successful career. Did all of my past problems get fixed? No, they didn't, but God told me to leave those things behind and press toward the mark for the prize of the high calling of God in Christ Jesus (Philippians 3:14, KJV).

I believe He is telling all of us to do this same thing. Although my past life was painful, I regret none of it. I thank God for it. If I had not gone through those things, I could not bless someone with my testimony. It's not over until God says it's over. He can make something out of nothing. Just because you may have come from mess doesn't mean you have to stay in mess or that your life has to continue to be messy. Is my life perfect now? I'd be lying to you if I said it was. As I write this, my husband and I are separated after 19 years of marriage. I lost my father to colon cancer in 2009; my mother and I were estranged for the past three years. Yes, I go through struggles daily. The enemy tries to bring those negative feelings of being unwanted, feeling unloved and insignificant back in my face again but I have to remember 2 Corinthians 5:17, *"Therefore if any man be in Christ, he is a new creature: old things are passed away; behold, all things are become new."*

The difference between how I handle my struggles now versus then is that I know I'm not alone. I don't have to fall back into my old ways to help me through my problems. I'm a part of a church family full of imperfect people with testimonies just like mine. They help me when I'm down by reminding me of God's promises and His goodness. They pray for me. This is the true definition of what a Christian is. None of us are perfect and all of us have skeletons in our closet. A true Christian exposes their mess and uses their testimony to encourage other people and give the glory to God. My Heavenly Father also carries my baggage for me. I no longer have to pull a U-Haul truck full of problems behind me. When I'm feeling overburdened I remember 1 Peter 5:7 which says, *"Cast all your anxiety on him because he cares for you."*

Whatever you are going through, whatever hurts, pains, and tragedies you carry with you, God already knows about them. He is just waiting for you to realize that you can't get through it on your own. He's waiting for you to ask for help. You are not alone in this life, even though it may feel like it sometimes. Those things that happened to you happened for a reason. That's not the end of you. To have a testimony you have to be tested. Be still and listen for His voice. It may not be audible but an inner voice that pushes you toward good. Repent for the things you know you are doing wrong and even those things you don't yet know are wrong and stop doing them. The Lord is waiting to save you and His arms are wide open. Tomorrow is not promised to us. Do it today. So, why are you waiting? If you don't know Christ as your personal Lord and Savior, pray this prayer:

God be merciful to me, a messed up soul. I believe Jesus Christ died for me and I believe that His precious blood will cleanse me from my sins. By faith, I now receive the Lord Jesus Christ into my heart; trusting Him to save my soul from going to hell. In Jesus name I pray, Amen!

You might not know the significance of this prayer, but God does. Get praying friends. Get in the family of God, a good church. You will be so glad you did. God didn't create us to live alone on this Earth. He meant for us to go through things so we can help each other through things. Never stop trying to live for God. Keep on moving. We are more than Conquerors! May God bless you along this journey.

Who shall separate us from the love of Christ? Shall trouble or hardship or persecution or famine or nakedness or danger or sword? As it is written: "For your sake we face death all day long; we are considered as sheep to be slaughtered. No, in all these things we are more than conquerors through him who loved us. For I am convinced that neither death nor life, neither angels nor demons, neither the present nor the future, nor any powers, neither height nor depth, nor anything else in all creation, will be able to separate us from the love of God that is in Christ Jesus our Lord." (Roman 8:35-39)

Carmencita Hughes

Carmencita D. Hughes was born in Fort Bragg, North Carolina. She spent most of her life in Indianapolis, IN with 12 of her adult years in California. She was born again on January 1st, 1983 under the late Bishop Morris E. Golder. However, she grew up in the Lord at Riverside Faith Temple under the late Apostle Joseph Sims and now Bishop Beatrice Sims, in Riverside California.

Evangelist Carmencita received her calling in 1994, but did not accept it until 2004. In 2006, she ministered under Pastor Ivory at Faith AME Church, Restoration Worship Center under Pastor Douglas James, and then, The Mercy Seat under Pastor Eric and Co-Pastor Timeko Whitaker. Currently, she is serving on the Evangelistic team at It Is Well Church, under Pastors Beverly and Reginal Barney. Her mission is to grow in the purpose that God has for her, wholeheartedly without fail.

She has received a Bachelor Degree in Business Administration from Martin Center University and her Associates in Applied Science in Computer Technology from Purdue University. In addition, she has completed the 5D 1-Day self-awareness seminar with Authentic Identity Coaching, LLC.

(Continued at conclusion of chapter)

CHAPTER THREE

Hallelujah Anyhow

Raw and uncut. I am a plain "Jane," a good old girl who was not saved from hard drugs, molestations, or abuse, but after getting saved, fell victim to fornication, church hurt, and deception. I had lacked networking skills, but was waiting for someone to reach out and pursue me and help me grow in the Lord, but was sought out for the wrong reason. It would have been nice to have the cushy easy life free of hardships but that was not how this scenario played out. Some of it was by choice, most of it by God's design. No one to blame, but My Hallelujah Anyhow paved the way throughout my salvation.

My story begins my freshman year in college. I lived in a hut style dorm, which housed about sixteen girls. My dorm was comprised of rich and wealthy young ladies, including some valedictorians in the mix. Our different backgrounds did not prevent us from growing close and looking out for one another. We had drinking parties almost every weekend. At least this was the norm when I was on campus. Fine men, plenty of liquor and lots of sex is what I looked forward to after a hard week of studying. Living for the weekend was me. I'm here to tell you, this lifestyle is not without consequence. Once while out of my mind intoxicated, I left the party I was attending alone. I was unaware there was a rapist on campus. My friends looked for me, and found me in a tree, in front of my dorm.

Although I do not remember that night, I thank God for His protection in the midst of my mess. It could have been worse. Finals were coming up and my weekend lifestyle started affecting my study habits. I needed some help. The guy I was dating was very intelligent, and used pills to help him study. He was smart and my boyfriend, what could it hurt? I tried the pills. By the end of that semester, I not only was taking pills but also smoked marijuana and drank heavily. Praise God, for His Grace, which got me through the semester.

Life Changing Turn

On New Year's Eve 1982, my life took an unexpected life-changing turn. My girlfriend from high school invited me to church. She got saved in high school, but never pushed me. I saw the change but was "whatever," that's good for her. When she invited me to church, my first thought was, "REALLY? Yeah right." I wanted to party. I reconsidered and thought, "Why not do something different for New Year's Eve, other than the norm?" Off to church I went without a clue what God had planned for me. The night progresses with good music, awesome singing, and remarkable testimonies. However, I was just there to do something different, with no idea of how different this night was going to be. As I sat in the balcony enjoying the atmosphere, I looked up and my best friend appeared and grabbed my hand. I did not notice she came from the choir stand. She looked into my eyes, with tears streaming down and said, "I know you want to be saved." At that moment, my body trembled and tears rolled down my cheeks. I could hear what she was saying but there was another voice. This voice was hysterical and desperate rehearsing in my ear the life and the so called "fun" I was having. The voice was reminding me of the men and the distinctive categories of satisfaction and fun I would miss out on, if I got saved. Then a clear, strong, smooth, silky, calm voice silenced the other voice and said: "This Is It; It is Time." So I took the walk down the long aisle. So many tears were falling, cleansing me from my past. I did not realize when my friend turned me into the hands of altar workers who got me ready to be baptized. As I came up out of that water, after going down in Jesus Name, I felt light as a feather. I did not understand the meaning behind all that was happening, but I knew it was God. The ladies told me to thank God. As I thanked God, I felt something take over my tongue and my body, and I spoke in tongues as the spirit gave utterance on January 1st, 1983. After reading Acts 2:38, I realized that my experience was identical to what happened on the Day of Pentecost. God gave me grace, and welcomed me into His Kingdom. This begins my journey as a child of God.

As a newborn babe in Christ, I started out in a big church, and my Bishop would say, "When you fall down, do not wobble in your mess; get up. Just being in the process of getting up, the victory begins. I knew I had issues. Men were my weakness. I had a man for every mood and need. Not that I was sleeping with all of them, but my circle included good company and protectors. Reminder, old mindsets do not automatically change after you are born again (saved), although some things change immediately. I already knew about the Ten Commandments, and that sex outside of marriage was not right for anyone, in or out of church. Being born again, made me feel like a virgin again.

The Church Hurt and Deception

I started my new life out with explosive testimonies and praise unto the Lord every chance I got. I had that uncontrollable, untamed fire for the Lord. Two sisters told me that the fire will die down, but hold onto the string and never let go. I was hungry for more. However, I did not know I was the target of church predators. I was fresh meat, prime for picking. Looking back, I felt my so called brothers in Christ were all lining up to see who was going to "hit it" first. Who will be the lucky one to get in her bed? I had an athletic body, and kept it tight and fit. My first encounter was with a minister. Yeah, he was fine from head to toe, flawless. Talk about singing, this man had a nice moving and sexy voice…. Yes, his singing and he was a minister too? Have mercy! I got to be real. I knew my weakness, but determined not to fall into his sinful ways. However, I thought his position in the church was my safety net. How wrong I was. He made a few advances on the first outing. I had finer men in my life, and they worked for it, so I was not that infatuated, but turned off. I kept my distance from that point. The next one up to bat befriended me first. I grew to like him, not knowing he had an agenda of his own. I fell hard for this man. After the sexual encounter, he told me that a deacon once told him that if you fall, then fall to sex. Okay, so this is how they do it in the church? I can continue get what I like, how I like it and still be saved. Wow! This is better than chocolate! Not knowing how messed up my thinking was, I straddled the fence and risked everyday of being spit out of God's mouth. (Revelation 3:16) Thank God for Grace.

Still messed up in pregnant again thinking, I went back to school and got pregnant. Abortion was my only option because I did not want to bear that shame in church nor quit school. You would think I learned my lesson. Nope! I was pregnant again after my third year in college. I scheduled another abortion. One week before my appointment, I got into a car accident. My car was hit so hard, that it flipped over the median to the other side of the highway landing on its side. My mother told me I was hanging from the roof of the car with blood all over my face. Two ministers, whom I never met, saw the accident and prayed for me at the scene. She did not know if I was dead or alive. I was taken to a small town hospital. While in the emergency room, I could see myself on the bed and people in the room. There, I felt no pain in my body as I watched them work on me. However, I woke up in a lot of pain asking about the baby. I was in my first trimester and positive the baby did not survive. Against all odds, I was still pregnant. My head was swollen to twice its size. Brain trauma was ruled out but there could be possible memory loss. In a moment of lucidity, I asked my best friend to make sure I kept that appointment. That same voice that spoke to me on January 1, 1983 spoke again saying, "I did not take your life, do not take this life." I obeyed and did not have the abortion. God's mercy and grace kept me during the months of recovery, the pregnancy and the normal delivery of a healthy baby boy.

Lesson learned, right? Life back on track with the Lord, right? Nope! Two more babies out of wedlock. I had another abortion and a tubal pregnancy in between these births. Yes, I knew that God's forgiveness is limitless, but I did not want to keep taking the chance of going to hell. The devil used that to make it seem okay to keep me doing what I was doing. Rationalizing my sin, I thought it was better to marry than to burn. That's what the bible said. I did not like the shame of going to church pregnant, but always wanted that inspirational music and preaching, which allowed me to endure the shame, and get a deposit of the Word in my heart. Therefore, a day before I had my third child, I got married without counsel or advice from anyone in the church or any of my friends.

This marriage became a disaster. We were unequally yoked. He was not saved and I prayed that he wanted to be. I was saved and wanted to live right. You think it would have balanced itself out. He was abusive in every sense of the word. He abused my mind, my body, and social life. Instead of having verbal fights, he preferred that I hit him. When I hit him, he complained I hit too hard and hit me back. Then, the battles began. I didn't win the battles, but I left a mark each time. At some point I got tired and refused to fight anymore, but my spouse kept the physical abuse going to the point of keeping me in check. It wasn't long after an encounter of the physical abuse, my husband raped me. We lived in a housing complex that was still building houses. I ran out of the house from him one night. He caught me on a hill, wrestled my clothes off, raped me, and then pushed me to the ground when he was done. I would have preferred for him to beat me half to death, to avoid that everlasting shame of being raped. I have never felt so violated by something I could not wash away. Being raped by someone who is supposed to love and protect you is another level of violation. I had moved out of state, away from family and friends, to be with this man. There was no one for me to confide in. His actions remained a secret to everyone but God; I talked to Him. My relationship with Him grew. He heard my cries on behalf of my husband, our marriage and our children. The marriage ended. The abuse was not God's will but the growth and lessons learned were. Then after the divorce, I found myself in a situation to find out this man considered me the most spiritual person he knew, and needed my help. I had to swallow my negative feelings, when God told me to help him. Through obedience, I was blessed. This was my true faith and trust developing to be totally used by Him, in spite of me.

Hallelujah Anyhow Begins

Finding myself single again was not easy. I had to face my sexual desires. God's love for me was never a doubt in my mind. I had more deposits, and knew God loved me, and wanted me His way. At this point, I had developed a mindset of just getting into the kingdom. As soon as I thought that, and through my weakness, I was pregnant again. Yes, I had another abortion. I was getting tired of the fight! Then my sister, who was on drugs, called me a "sanctified hoe." My life was this revolving door that I couldn't escape. I convinced myself that because of the abortions, the sexual desires, and inability to give myself wholeheartedly to God, I felt hopeless and unworthy. I decided to leave the church. This is where my Hallelujah Anyhow begins.

So, I was ready to let go and go back, but God let me see He was not ready to let me go! HALLELUJAH! He allowed me to see my life without Him in it. The devastation that could have been, should have been, and would have been, had He not been present in my life. HALLELUJAH ANYHOW!

I was walking backwards, looking at my past trying to move forward but only going back to what was familiar and easy. I was focused on the abortions, sexual relationships, birthing children out of wedlock...looking back...walking backwards. I had to stop drowning in my sin, and allowing the devil to use the abortions and sexual desires to keep me from what God has called me to do. Then, God simply let me know that He loved me so much that He was with me before the time I accepted Him through that moment, and every day. He was only waiting for me to turn my focus to Him. The things I involved myself in were not a deterrent of His love, care and concern for me. He still had a plan for my life. He still desired a relationship with me. Not one of my previous relationships changed His mind or desire to take me in His arms and be the Lover of my soul. What manner of love is this? I stopped trying to comprehend the love and make myself worthy, and just accept the love. This is where restoration begins in my journey to the Kingdom.

Restoration and the Mercy Seat

My relationship with Him changed. The door of that dark ugly place I felt trapped in was opened by the light of His love. He deemed me worthy of redemption, from the strong holds in my life. All things became shadows in the light of His love for me. The way I saw myself changed. My words about myself changed. Truth replaced all the lies I believed about myself. Deliverance came to my spirit, soul and body.

Ultimately through it all, I attended church throughout my imperfections. I surrendered to be the clay of the Potter, and my Father molded me into what He wants me to be. Hallelujah Anyhow is a song by Thomas Whitfield. The words are simple but they have kept me on the path of redemption. I've learned a few trials could come; a few things could come that may put me off course; a few things could even knock me down, but He taught me to say, Hallelujah Anyhow. I changed my mindset to: The more Hallelujah Anyhows I give up to the Lord, sin will be depleted and I will win the war. The devil had made my sin so great in my head, that I felt unworthy to deliver God's ultimate Glory in my life. I internalized that sin is sin, and no sin is greater than the other in God's eyes. I was redeemed, and now a winner destined for eternal life with my Lord and Savior Jesus Christ. This was my restoration and eventual encounter with the mercy seat of God.

> *Do not allow the devil to help internalize your sin, but instill scriptures and your Hallelujah Anyhow, as you journey to the Kingdom of God.*

My relationship with God saved my life! Through this relationship I was able to make the 180 degree turn to see my future. My past is now behind me not in front of me. Hallelujah Anyhow not only got me through my imperfections, but gets me through what I may think is wrong or unfair. I do know that God will do "exceedingly abundantly above all that I can ever ask or think "(Ephesians 3:20). Looking back, my God has done it then, and is still doing it now. So that string I was told to hold onto from those two ladies in 1983, kept me destined for eternal existence in the Kingdom. To-day, I am living heaven on earth as Evangelist Carmencita D. Hughes. So, although I have not experienced extensive drug abuse, molestation, or even abandonment, the bottom line is Hallelujah Anyhow for all things encountered. Do not allow the devil to help internalize your sin, but instill scriptures and your Hallelujah Anyhow, as you journey to the Kingdom of God. It is not in vain that things have occurred, by the decisions we make, but to God be the Glory for what he has done. So it is well, for ALL the GLORY belongs to God.

You have heard my story. I now ask, "Is there anything too hard for God?" Now, it's your turn. Look over your shoulder. What do you see? Whatever it is, it is behind you. That is your past. Look at it one more time and shout at the top of your lungs, "HALLELUJAH ANYHOW!" This is your time and your season to move forward without hindrance. Your Hallelujah Anyhow moment is now! Seize it!

BIOGRAPHY CONTINUED

Evangelist Carmencita D. Hughes is the mother of 3: 1 son, and 2 daughters. The significant influences in her spiritual growth: the late Bishop Morris E. Golder; Beatrice Jackson (spiritual mother); and Minister Douglas James, who has been her pastor, but always been that brother, who reminded her of whose she was in the midst of all the storms.

Carmencita retired from the United States Army in 2013. She learned, and still carries the Army Core Values of Loyalty, Duty, Respect, Selfless-Service, Honor, Integrity and Personal Courage, into her journey in fulfilling God's predestined purpose in her life. The Bible says, The steps of a good man are ordered by the Lord, And He delights in His Way (Psalms 37:23) So, it is time, to not just walk in those steps, but to continually operate in that calling for the Kingdom of God.

Leslie Ann Wesley

Christian, servant, public speaker, entrepreneur, world changer, social activist, vision coach, community organizer, innovator, advocate, and change agent are just a few words that effectively describe Leslie Wesley.

Leslie is passionate about helping individuals find their greatest potential. The Indiana University of Bloomington alumna is a credible and experienced consultant in her native city of South Bend, Indiana. She specializes in youth development, parent education, entrepreneurship, workshop training, after-school, extended day, and summer learning.

Aside from her dedication to developing and implementing programs to enhance student life, Leslie Wesley shares her passion for community service endeavors, by leading students in a community service project preparation and implementation programs for underserved and underrepresented students in South Bend. . Leslie is also the Co-Founder of Reposition Inc. Reposition Inc. provides leadership training, financial literacy coaching, and life coaching.

(Continued at conclusion of chapter)

CHAPTER FOUR

Abundant Life

I dedicate this chapter to my wonderful mother An-nell Waters. A true Woman of God. I thank God every day for choosing you as my mother.

My four beautiful children...Jazmine, Taylor, Derrick Jr. and Blake...I love you all so much. My heartbeats.

To my wonderful loving husband Derrick Sr., you are my Rock. God granted me favor when he choose you as my husband. Your love for me is unconditional. I love you my BOAZ...

For nothing is forever, but the Love of God lasts forever...

In 1970 George (Georgie) met his father, Lester

George loved Lester

Lester loved George, unconditionally.

They shared an enduring bond

Our Heavenly Father saw fit to never let them be separated,

As they lived together in love, they left together in love

On Monday, March 6, 2000

The Lord whispered their names

Knowing how much both loved each other

He gathered them in his arms as one

The bond remains unbroken....

I felt as if the world had cracked apart, and the noise was deafening. My father and brother had slipped through a chasm so big that they were gone forever. I could not take it all in; instead, my mind felt filled with white noise. It blocked out the actual words spoken to me; it blocked out all my thoughts but the most basic impulses to keep breathing, ask questions, do the next thing in front of me. Although I was not present at the time of the car accident that killed my father and brother, I can see now that the violence of a single instant rippled throughout my life and the life of my family, just like a sonic boom.

The Nightmare

We do our best to prepare for everything in life. As Christians, we live every day as an opportunity to make peace, hear God's voice, and prepare ourselves for a new life in Jesus. Just a day before, my children had spent a happy Sunday afternoon with my parents. I had left church and gone straight to a friend's house where we stuffed envelopes for an upcoming fundraiser. When I arrived at my parents' house, my dad was seated in his favorite chair. He looked satisfied, almost serene, as he watched my children rush to greet me. I asked him how he was doing, even though I thought I could guess his answer.

"I'm doing fine, Les Ann," he said. "And I joined the choir."

"The choir?!" I laughed.

He smiled. "Yes, the choir. I've been singing."

"Daddy," I said, "you haven't joined no choir." But yes, he insisted, he had joined the church choir. There was something different in his tone and it made me pause. Always a humble and gentle man, my father sounded content with a quiet joy. I asked my children to give their grandpa a kiss so we could take our leave. With the simple act of saying goodbye, I had the last glimpse of my father's face.

Later I realized that joining the choir was another step in my father's journey toward leaving this world. While God was preparing my father to become the angel I always knew him to be, on that soft, simple day, God was preparing me, too. However, I was not ready to listen. I was not prepared for the storm that followed the next day.

On March 6th, 2000, it was a slightly "off" day. I felt unwell. As a mother of two young children, ages twenty-one months and three, I stayed home from work and did paperwork. While my children played with their toys on the floor, I finally put down my head and rested on the couch.

When the phone rang, I answered and was surprised to hear my mother's neighbor on the other end. She stated that my dad and brother had been in a car accident only a few blocks away. A fender bender, I thought. Can't be a big deal. "It's bad," the neighbor said. "It's real bad." My body reacted before my thoughts began. I started to shake uncontrollably and then cajoled her for more information. She said, "You need to get here, Leslie. You need to get here."

As I paced the floor, my voice rose. "What's wrong? Tell me. What's wrong?" I tried to call everyone, anyone, in attempts to get more information. Without it, I felt blind. Lost. Terror bloomed inside of my chest. When another neighbor called, she told me that one person in the car was unresponsive. At that point, I knew my world had fallen to pieces.

I fell to my knees and sobbed. Even though my neighbor remained on the phone, I began an internal dialogue with God. Please, I begged. This cannot be true. I am sick and must have fallen asleep, so this must be a dream. Please, God, let this be a nightmare, the worst of my life. After all, I saw my dad only yesterday. I heard the quiet joy in his voice as he told me about the choir. I watched him kiss my children goodbye, each kiss a blessing on their smooth, salty foreheads.

Numbed

When I arrived at the hospital, my mother and other family were already there. By then I knew my father had died at the scene of the accident, but my brother still had a chance. He was in surgery. We all clung to the hope of his survival like passengers in life boats, watching our ship sink under the waves. I rocked myself and cried. Why us? I thought. Why me? And my dad, why didn't I have time to say goodbye? Why hadn't I spent more time with him? Hadn't I known that I would lose him someday?

When the surgeon informed us that my brother had died in surgery, I fell into my mom's arms and then slipped onto my knees, unable to move. However, my thoughts and tears were a hot fury. Right there in the midst of my family, I began a cycle of rage, remorse, questioning God, wanting vengeance, and then wanting forgiveness. Most of all, I wanted answers. Why had the other driver been so careless? Why was he alive and my father dead? At the time, I thought answers would end my agony.

We do our best to prepare ourselves. Intellectually, we understand that death is a part of life on Earth. However, I had talked to my father only the day before.

That memory was too fresh and this horror in the hospital was too raw. Our lives had split apart, and without my father, my world no longer made sense.

Even though I was far from accepting or even understanding what had happened, I got up off my knees both literally and figuratively. I felt numb and deaf, but many practical considerations needed my attention. Before we left the hospital, there were forms and decisions. Then it seemed that we never caught our breath before we had other matters to decide. Who would notify all of the family? Where were life insurance policies and other documents? What kind of casket should we choose? Although many people flocked to help my family, I was only dimly aware of them. At the same time, I felt the need to be grateful. However, the numbness never left me. I had already lost two sisters, so I was no stranger to death. But without my father, nothing made sense in the world. The world had stopped; at one point, it even felt as if my heart had stopped. I walked through my world like a stranger.

Suffocating Sorrow

"For I am the Lord, your God, who takes hold of your right hand and says to you, Do not fear; I will help you." (Isaiah 41:13)

Help me, Jesus. I cry to you from this dark place. Everything in my life is blackness, heaviness, sadness. My joy in life is gone; my hope for the future is gone. I lay immobilized day after day, unable to move, to function, unable to care for my children.

Where are you, Lord? Why don't you come and rescue me? I cannot help myself. I cannot even pray or hear your voice. Lift me out of this deep pit. I have tried to find my way out. I've tried to cry my way out, to scream my way out. I am exhausted. Unless you help me, I am finished.

If this testing place is from you, God teach me what it is you would have me learn. Cover me with your grace and your mercy. Help me; Father I need you. Please help me breath through this suffocating sorrow. Send your answer, God. Take me by the hand and restore me. Restore my life and restore my soul. I'm trusting you Lord. Help me!!!!!!!!!!!!!!!

Life After The Storm

"Who shall separate us from the Love of Christ"

(Romans 8:35)

Although I was familiar with the stages of grief as described by Elisabeth Kubler-Ross, the sudden loss of my father and brother seemed too devastating for anything sensible to penetrate my pain. Looking back, I can see that the stages gave me a framework for survival and helped me clarify what felt like a tornado of feelings and thoughts. Even the awful, cold numbness of denial allowed me to take small steps at first. I got off my knees. I took care of my mother, children, and others who needed comfort. I walked through those terrifying arrangements and decisions. Next, anger gave me back my power. I could move back and forth between numb

Help me, Jesus. I cry to you from this dark place. Everything in my life is blackness, heaviness, sadness. My joy in life is gone; my hope for the future is gone. I lay immobilized day after day, unable to move, to function, unable to care for my children.

denial and hot anger in only a few hours. Dimly, I realized that I was moving along a path, even if I felt out of control and helpless.

However, if I had not learned to depend on God, I would never have weathered the storm of that week. Prayer and scripture kept my heart soft when it wanted to shrivel with pain and anger. My faith connected me to spirit when I longed to withdraw in sadness.

I'm Free

Don't grieve for me, for now I'm free
I'm following the path God for me,
I took His hand when I heard Him call
I turned my back and left it all.
I could not stay another day
To laugh, to love to work or play.
Tasks left undone must stay that way
I found that place at the close of the day

If my parting has left a void,
Then fill it with remembered joy.
A friendship shared, a laugh, a kiss,
Ah yes, these things, I too will miss

Perhaps my time seemed all too brief,
Don't lengthen it now with undue grief,
Lift up your heart and share with me
God wanted me now; He has set me free.
God was saying to me... Move on Leslie and let them go.

The Path to Understanding & Forgiveness

Dear God,

It's me... Help me to forgive...... Grant me with the gift of forgiveness. Amen

Matthew 6:12, *And forgive us our debts, as we forgive our debtors.*

This word forgiveness has been debated from generation to generation. The problem is not the definition of the word; it is the execution of the word. We know what forgive means but how to perform it becomes a journey. We're not talking about forgiving someone for money, a mishap or a mistake. How do you forgive someone who changed your destiny? How do forgive someone who changed your direction, your dynamics? Someone who affected your walk, your ways, your worship? It is easy to forgive someone for rolling their eyes at you, stepping on your toe or not speaking to you. But how do you forgive someone who wrecked your past, rearranged your present and revoked your promise.

The word "forgive" in Greek is "aphiemi," which means to "Let go." It paints the picture of divorce. We have associated divorce with just paperwork. But have you ever met someone who was divorced on paper but not in their mind.

Divorced – changed your name, changed your look but you didn't change your mind. You changed your address, changed the way you dress but you didn't change your heart. That is why first time marriages have a 50% rate of divorce but 2nd time marriages have a 65% divorce rate because the debtor has not been forgiven; he or she has been replaced with another debtor!

Divorce means "to separate, to sever," not just on paper but mentally as well! Because remember Christ is talking about ministry. How do I spiritually separate from my debtor when I remember what they did to me?

When you forgive your debtor you legally and mentally separate from the pain and all power and control the pain has over you. You know if someone hasn't truly forgiven their debtor because when you hear them tell the story, you think it happened yesterday. Their eyes get teary; their voice trembles; their stomach gets weak, and their head begins to hurt. That is because they have not released the control the pain that the debtor caused has on them.

But both God and the debtor cannot have control over you! We know how to file the paper for forgiveness but we don't know how to mentally forgive. We can't only file the physical paperwork; we have to file the emotional paperwork too! When you get back control of your mind, you will find out that the pain itself was not physical but emotional. They look the same but they are not.

Physical pain can stop you from walking, talking, eating and sleeping and emotional pain looks as if it can stop you from walking, talking, eating and sleeping. But emotional pain cannot stop you from walking; emotional pain cannot stop you from talking; it cannot stop you from eating and it cannot stop you from sleeping. It can only stop your desire to walk, talk, eat or sleep. When you release the pain caused by your debtor, your appetite changes!

If I were to reverse the text it would read as we forgive our debtors forgive us our debts.

The reason why we should forgive is because we cannot receive forgiveness for our debts unless we first forgive our debtors. God is not taking excuses but He only wants evidence.

The two words "forgive" have the same meaning but the syntax is different. The first "forgive" is in the imperative mood which means "to make a request." The second forgive is in the indicative mood which is "an evidential mood or statement of fact."

There has to be evidence that you forgave the debtor in order for you to request the debts you owe God to be forgiven by God. Once you say you forgive someone you are accountable for such a thing. People say they have forgiven others, but you can't fool God, the one who made our ears. Do you think he can hear? The one that gave you eyes; do you think He can see? What evidence is sufficient for God?

But I say unto you, Love your enemies, bless them that curse you, do good to them that hate you, and pray for them which despitefully use you, and persecute you. Matt 5:44 (KJV)

Faith-Hope-Love

We have faith to believe that God is our creator and that His son, Jesus came into this world for the primary purpose of dying on the cross, shedding His blood, paying our sin debt in full and making it possible for everyone who believes to have eternal life. But do we have the faith to believe that God is able to take care of everything?

As believers, our actions are seen by those ready to cast doubt on our Faith and those with questions about salvation. I clearly understand as there was a time when I questioned my beliefs. But I know, you can only be a Christian if Christ is in you. Without a strong foundation you can easily lose hope. You see I always knew the word of God, but it's different when you have to go through trials in order to demonstrate what God has instilled in you.

We have an awesome responsibility to live a life of excellence. Matthew 12:33 says, *"Make a tree good and its fruit will be good, or make a tree bad, and its fruit will be bad, for as tree is recognized by his fruits."*

We should all want to bring good fruit. I realize that that part of my healing process was the fact that I was starting to walk in Godliness. As many say, we are the only bible some people will ever see. That is why I let everyone around me know how good God is and how he has blessed me over and over again. I let everyone know there is no greater love than the love of God. God has done so much for me and He can do the same for you. What is love? God is! I let everyone know there is no greater love than the love of my God. The wisdom I share comes from the word of God and many years of experience trusting God and believing He has a plan for me. The word clearly states in Jeremiah 29:11, "For I know the plans I have for," declares the Lord, "plans to prosper you and not to harm you, plans to give you hope and a future." It is because of my Faith in God's word, and the confidence I have in His plan for my life that I trust He will do what He said He would do. The Word clearly reminds us daily that our loving God will direct our path when we learn to trust Him with all of our heart and acknowledge His word in everything that we do.

Remember, it is your responsibility to share God's love with others so that at the end of your life you will know you made a difference in someone's life. Share with someone else, your abundant life!

...But I do not want you to be ignorant, brethren, concerning those who have fallen asleep, lest you sorrow as others who have no hope.

For if we believe that Jesus died and rose again, even so God will bring with Him those who sleep in Jesus.

1Thessalonians 4:13-14

BIOGRAPHY CONTINUED

Leslie is happily married to her husband of 23 years, Derrick Wesley, Sr. She is the 8th of 11 children, and the proud mother of Jazmine, Taylor, Derrick Jr, and Blake Wesley. When she is not in mommy and wife mode, Leslie is out in the community volunteering. Leslie is a member of the Drifters Inc., The Links, Incorporated, and the Junior League of South Bend. Her list of awards include the Michiana Make a Difference Award and the 2016 Community Trailblazer Award. She is also a proud member of Greater Saint John Missionary Baptist Church in South Bend Indiana.

Leslie is a "Servant" for God. Her heart is to serve others in a way where God gets the glory out of everything she does.

Tedria Denise

Tedria Denise was born
and raised in Harvey, IL.
Searching for love in the
wrong places led her to have
her first of 5 children at the
age of 15. Becoming a teen
mother quickly changed her
perspective on life.

She worked hard not to become
a stereotypical teenage mother. She graduated with
honors and was accepted in the Who's Who Among
High School students for her achievements. She eventually earned her BS in Business Management from
Indiana Wesleyan University. Tedria served in the area
of special education within the school systems of South
Bend, Indiana, and Indianapolis, Indiana for over 17
years. She has served in various church leadership
roles. Her employment history is complimentary of
her multitudes of talent. She loves to sew, write, draw,
teach, and watch movies. She also loves to sing and
dance even though her family teases her about her lack
of talent in those areas. She is an entrepreneur, Certified 5D Identity Coach, Certified Human Behavior
Consultant and author of "I Arise, I Arise, Against All
Odds, I Arise." Tedria is currently in graduate school.

CHAPTER FIVE

The Pursuit of Radical Faith

Why is my faith so radical? Understand this, behind every strong person of faith is an even stronger testimony; a testimony of how life drug them to their lowest and left them with only their belief in God. The trials we experience are designed to draw us closer to God. They are designed to reveal all that He is, and all that He desires to do in our lives. Each and every trial we face serve two purposes. At first, we learn from them. Next, we teach from them. Never in a million years would I have imagined I would become an author, a spiritual empowerment leader, and a life coach. In the words of Langston Hughes, "Life for me ain't been no crystal stair."

The things I have experienced made me feel less than worthy until I realized that my story was for His Glory. God gets the glory out of our stories when we learn our lessons, seek forgiveness for our wrongs, and then launch out in search of our brothers and sisters in Christ who are in dire need of our help. In order to do this, we must be in radical pursuit of God! In my pursuit, I daily disrupt the devil's agenda in my life and in my family's life by standing firm on the promises of God; no matter what the situation may seem like to my natural eye. I recruit others to join me in having this same type of radical faith. In this moment, I am recruiting you! That's right, you. As you read my story, think of your own. You've gone through a few storms, yet you stand. Hasn't God done enough to heighten your faith? Has He not opened doors? Has He not reached into your situations? Has he not been a healer and a deliverer? Even if you've not experienced His power in your own life, I'm sure that you've witnessed His greatness in the lives of those around you. I pray that by reading my story, you will understand why it is important to have radical faith in your radical pursuit of God!

Before I dive into my own story, I would like to discuss the story of Shadrach, Meshach, & Abednego found in Daniel 3:19-30. Many of you have heard this story in children's church, at Sunday School, or during a sermon. If you've never heard of this story, pick up a bible and check it out! I have often marveled at this story and wondered if I could ever be as strong, brave, and radical as Shadrach, Meshach & Abednego. The more I thought about this story and compared it to my own life, I realized that I too could have the same level of radical faith as these Hebrew boys. As a matter of fact, I exhibited this same faith throughout many of my life's most tumultuous obstacles.

> *God gets the glory out of our stories when we learn our lessons, seek forgiveness for our wrongs, and then launch out in search of our brothers and sisters in Christ who are in dire need of our help.*

You see, these three men had to make a decision against a direct order given by the king of their time. The king ordered everyone to bow down to a huge statue that was built of gold. Everyone around them did as the king ordered, but they refused to bow down and serve any other god but the God of Israel. Their faith was so strong that they were willing to die for what they believed. They were willing to die because they knew God had their backs.

Well, you know how the story goes. Someone ratted Shadrach, Meshach, and Abednego out to the king. The king was furious and demanded the three be thrown into a furnace of fire. The king wanted all the kingdom to see what happened to disobedient subjects. Before throwing them into the furnace, he gave them one more chance to defy their God and bow to his god. The three boldly refused. Wait. This is where many of us get confused. These men were offered what many would view as a ram in the bush, yet they still chose death over submission to an idol god. Was it really that serious? Couldn't they have bowed, preserved their lives and asked God for forgiveness later? Yes, and yes. These men of faith could have chosen the easy way out, but if they did, what would we have to read about as it relates to radical faith? It was just that serious! Let's get back to the story for just a moment.

After the three refused the king's request, the king became furious. He ordered that the fire in the furnace be turned up seven times hotter than it already was. The fire was so hot that the soldiers who threw the three men into the furnace fell dead from the heat. What happened next shows how their radical faith changed the heart of the king and made him a believer. When the king peered into the furnace, his eyes saw four bodies in the fire. The king, shocked by what he saw, demanded that the three men be pulled out of the furnace. Shadrach, Meshach, and Abednego emerged from the flames without any residue of the heat they had been thrown in. Their garments were untouched. The king knew then that the God of Israel was alive and worthy to be praised.

I don't know about you, but I have been thrown in the fire more times than I wish to count. My life started off beautiful. I was a happy little girl, living in a beautiful two story home with my brother and both parents. Things were great. My father worked hard and provided the very best for our family. My brother and I enjoyed things that most children our age and race were not privileged to experience. Life took a gut wrenching turn when I turned seven. At an innocent age, I was sexually molested by a relative. In fear of what my father would do to him, I kept his dirty secret. To put the icing on the cake, my mother was being abused by my father and eventually packed us up and took us on an unstable, house hopping adventure to freedom. I had known of my father's abusiveness, so I was proud of my mother for running away. She became my hero. At first, our adventure was fun. We stayed in a hotel, then hopped around to the homes of my mother's friends. Unfortunately, this unstable freedom ruined my childhood and my relationship with my mother. We had been kicked to the curb so many times, that I began to wish we were back at home with my father. Instead of enjoying my childhood, I took on the responsibility of protecting both my younger brother, and my mother.

Over a course of time, my hero became selfish, man-crazy, and unsupportive. I still cringe at the thought of the horrible men she dated. From being asked by one of her lovers to engage in a threesome with them, to having to stand up to one of her abusive boyfriends, life got ridiculously crazy. For the life of me, I could not understand why my mother allowed men to become her kryptonite. I remember crying out to her as a teenager, and doing crazy things just to get her attention. I would often attempt to cut myself and scream out absurdities. My mother, knowing that I was only acting out for attention, ignored my cries. This of course drove me to seek love from a young man who only desired sexual intimacy. He was not capable of loving my broken pieces the way I needed him to. Even though I knew he was not to me what I needed, his sexual attention was better than no attention. Since I couldn't get the love and attention I desired from my mother, I settled for an imitation of love. My self-value and self worth was diminished because of it. I soon became a teen mom of two, struggling to graduate from high school.

As if the furnace couldn't get any hotter, my mom refused to support me and my children. So on top of being a single teen mom, I was left alone to provide for myself and my children the best way I knew how. Right when things seemed unbearable, God sent an angel who opened the door for me to get stable housing and a job. Through it all, I remained optimistic and fought to turn my life around. I emerged from the furnace a high school graduate determined to make a better life for my children. Apparently, this wasn't enough for the enemy. So he tested my radical faith once again.

After graduating from high school, I moved from the busy life of inner-city Illinois to South Bend, in hopes of creating a better childhood for my children than what I had experienced. In South Bend, I met a guy I had dated in inner-city Illinois. He too had moved to South Bend. We soon became serious in our rekindled relationship. One day while walking downtown with the kids, we were invited into a newly built church. We had nothing to do, so we went in. We had an amazing experience. Our family became faithful and consistent members. Our relationship grew. I grew closer to God, but he, on the other hand could not leave the fast life. He refused to be sold out for Christ the way I wanted to be. I eventually told him that he needed to decide if he wanted to serve God and be with me or stay in the streets and leave. That following Sunday, he showed up for church. He became more consistent in his pursuit of Christ. Seeing that we had children out of wedlock, we began to consider marriage. My children were not his, however, we never revealed that information to them. That year, we became the first couple the church joined in marriage. We were a young family, with no home to call our own. After we were married, I soon found out that I was pregnant. The church helped us find the services and resources needed to get a home. We put in application after application until finally we received a letter, but it wasn't an approval letter. It was a denial letter for a newly renovated townhome community. We were admonished to put in for an appeal. We won the hearing and God blessed us with a three bedroom townhome, all utilities paid except the water, which we received a waiver for. I was well into my pregnancy at that time and should have been on bed rest because I had been experiencing, horrible cramps, and some bleeding. I tried to move only when necessary, but I had to care for my children. My new husband had other issues that were more serious than I ever realized.

The night before our move, it snowed really bad. As I prepared our things for the move, I began to cramp. I decided to go to the hospital. They gave me an ultrasound, but they did not find anything wrong. They released me from the hospital, told me to rest, and come back if the pain continued or if the bleeding got worse. What they failed to tell me was that the pains I felt were labor pains and that my body was preparing to deliver my stillborn child. The next day, we walked to our new home from the shelter. We settled in, made a palette on the floor, and fell asleep. As we slept, my husband snuck out of the house, leaving me in my stressed pregnant state alone with two children.

In the middle of the night, I began to feel excruciating pain. I called for my husband, but he was no where to be found. I scrambled my way to the bathroom. I was in labor for hours throughout the night. I had the baby boy. He was the size of my hand. He dropped into a towel I had under me. All I can remember is seeing his limp little body. I couldn't see his details because my vision was blurred from crying. At that moment my heart and soul cried out even more to God. I wrapped my baby in the towel, and prayed that God would send someone to help me before the kids found me lying on the bathroom floor in a pool of blood. I was weak and unable to move. The sun rose and I became even more anxious because a gentleman from the new church we were attending was scheduled to pick us up. Thank God for thin walls. Our next door neighbor heard my voice and prayers as she was in her bathroom. She immediately came over. My oldest son, Shawn, woke up and opened the door. I heard the woman ask Shawn to stay downstairs as she ran up to check on me.

She came in and took charge as if she had known me forever. She called the ambulance, held my hand, prayed with me, and told me not to worry about the kids or anything else. The paramedics arrived, took the baby, and dropped him in a paper bag. They covered my nude bottom with blankets and rushed me to the hospital. I did not see my husband again until I was released from the hospital. I refused to lose my faith or be shaken by his actions. I chose to fight for my husband's soul and trust God in my marriage. Despite my attempt, my husband landed himself in and out of jail, finally leaving me with five children to care for alone. We divorced. In 2000, I was once again released from the furnace. God began to restore me and He rewarded my faithfulness.

Now, I pray you understand why my faith is so radical. I owe God my life. I could go on and on about the many times He has kept me. I can write for days about how He continuously delivered me from the furnace unblemished, no matter how hot the flames became. While the days of Shadrach, Meshach, and Abednego are long gone, I am a living testimony of what radical faith looks like. I pray that from my transparency, you have been motivated to keep the faith and press through in the name of our Lord and Savior Jesus Christ.

Take a moment and think about your own life. What are

you doing with your testimonies? Are you locking them up in fear of what people will think about what you have been through? Are you preserving them on the shelves of your mind and hiding them from the world? I don't know about you, but I refuse to let all that I have been through be in vain. The trick of the enemy isn't always in his crafty attacks. Sometimes, his tricks lie in your silence. Understand this: If the enemy can keep your lips sealed in shame and embarrassment, he can keep others bound in their transgressions. Who could benefit from your story? Who can be inspired by simply knowing that they are not alone? Now that you have been recruited to exhibit radical faith, will you in return recruit others? Having just wrote a memoir on my personal life story, I am well aware of the doubt the enemy is setting in your heart as you think about sharing your testimony with the world. "People will look at you funny. People won't believe you. Your story won't free anyone. It's best for you to just shut up." The enemy is the father of lies.

As you get in radical faith to ignite the faith of others, seek God's guidance. Ask Him to lead you to those who need to hear your story. Sometimes, people assume that ministry only happens from the pulpit. Your life should be your ministry. People should be able to see the way you live through the good, bad, and ugly and be inspired to persevere in Christ. Seek God's guidance on the platform in which He desires to use you. He may desire to use you in life groups, through blogs, through a book, through your church, or simply through your daily social media posts. There are many ways to share your testimony. No matter where God sends you to share your story, know that lives will be changed. I cannot begin to tell you the burden that has been lifted from my family through the release of my testimony. My children and I are closer than ever. They have a better understanding of why life happened the way it did for us.

I encourage you, child of God, to have radical faith in God.

I understand. Life has thrown so many unfair punches, your eyes have been blackened and your back has been broken. Even if you could see a way out, you feel as though you don't have the strength to move. Be encouraged. Know that as long as you have faith in God, you can continue to move forward. Keep getting up. Your current situation may be full of heartache, pain, and confusion. Continue to seek God. Stay faithful to His word, and stand firm on His promises. Your present state is not final. Your victory lies in your faith in God. He is the final Judge. The gavel is in His faithful hand. He knows the plans He has for your life because He created you. Everything you have endured has a purpose in the grand scheme. It may not make much sense now, but trust that He will bring you out of the furnace for all to see and believe that He is a mighty God worthy to be praised!

Let us pray,

Lord, please bless the families and generations connected to the person reading this book. Cover them and elevate them to their next level in life. May they live out their purpose. May you grant every desire you have placed in their hearts, in Jesus' name. Amen.

Author's Note: "There are many that do not understand me. They wonder why my FAITH is so strong and radical. Today, I share my heart and give you a taste of my testimony. I will share with you only one reflection of all I have experienced throughout life that contributes to my radical pursuit of God. I am impelled to show Christ in my life and to exhort others. I pray that my story not only exhorts, but touch the hearts of many across the nations. I pray that it brings hope and a pursuit of radical faith to all who reads it."

~ *Tedria Denise*

Deagria Cook

Deagria Cook is a public speaker, author, advocate, leader, and survivor. A servant at heart, Deagria life's goals are to assist others to live out loud, chase their dreams and to love and completely accept themselves.

Known on social media for her powerful inspiration videos; Deagria is currently the host of Life Lessons with Deagria, a show dedicated to bringing encouragement and hope on Zaahi Studios Network.
Deagria's career spans over a decade in the beauty industry. She now uses her talents and skills to empower, encourage, and motivate women and girls to live their best lives possible. Whether in front of an arena, or a small group she is invaluable and brings excitement. This highly dedicated and motivated professional uses her many gifts and talents to work as a change agent in her community. As an AmeriCorps Service member she works to support survivors of domestic violence and sexual assault across the greater Indianapolis area.

Born in Indianapolis, Deagria considers Los Angeles, California her home. Deagria has three adult children, is a military mom, and has a grandson. She enjoys public speaking, beauty and fashion, writing, and giving back to the community.

CHAPTER SIX

I'm Still Standing

This Little Miracle

The birth of a child should bring sounds of joy and laughter as the family gathers to celebrate. This was not the case in the spring of 1972 at Wishard Hospital. Freddie Mae and Norrell were being told their precious baby girl was going to die. The many doctors and well-meaning nurses were filling the atmosphere with hopeless remarks. "She won't make it." "If she does make it, she will be blind, retarded and will never walk." And lastly, "You'd better let her go." It was hard for both of them having to decide whether to allow their child to live with possible birth defects or allow her to die. I was that baby girl, born premature and only weighing in at one pound thirteen ounces.

My dad was nineteen years my mother's senior. He worked as a brick mason. Together, they had brought 5 children into this world. He was a protector not willing to let the opinions of the medical staff decide my fate, so he went home to pray.

My dad went home and bargained with my Father, God. I learned of this many years later. He prayed, "Lord, if you let our tiny girl live, I'll love and support, and protect her all the days of my life." God honored his prayer and my dad kept his promise.

I spent the first six months of my life in an incubator. When I reached six pounds my mom and dad were able to take me home. I believe God didn't just strengthen my body during those six months but He made me whole and equipped me for my life's journey. My physical development was delayed; I hadn't found a reason to yet smile and I suffered from chronic asthma, but I had survived! The doctors and nurses were proven wrong. God had a plan for my life; I had to live! To add to the miracle, the hospital bill was a whopping 75 cents, which my dad gladly paid for out of his pocket.

I finally found my smile around my first birthday. The next 13 years of my life were pretty normal. I felt loved and secure. Until one day...

Childhood's Sudden End

The muffled sounds of my parents' voice awakened me. They were having a quiet disagreement while lying in bed. Their voices raised just enough for me to hear my father curse at my mother and say, "I don't need you; what I need you for; and you can leave!" Where was this coming from? Who was this man? This was not the loving provider and protector I knew my dad to be. My life would never be the same.

A short time later my mom showed up at my school and announced, "We're moving to California in the morning; your father's not going; I'm leaving him." I was shocked. The next day I was told to put only what I needed into a trash bag. My pleading, screaming and sobbing had no effect on her. With my sister and one of her 4 children in the car, we left. I still see my father's face as she drove past him and blew the horn.

The drive to California was long, filled with uncertainty and fear. We finally arrived in Los Angeles just days before my 15th birthday. I think this birthday was a defining moment in my life. There was no party, no cake, no friends, no daddy. I felt like my life was over. My feelings weren't too far off. My sister got locked up and my mother was granted custody of her 4 children. At the age of 15 I became a surrogate mother to my nieces ages 11, 9, 5 and 2. I spent that summer adjusting to my new way of life.

Surviving Watts

We lived in Inglewood with my aunt. My high school was within walking distance. I was nervous because of the gang activity. The first lesson I learned at my new school was how to survive. I witnessed much gang violence that first day. Needless to say, when the school day came to an end, I was thankful to have lived through it.

My mother was finally able to get us our own place in the heart of Watts in South Central L.A. This was townhouse-style public housing with cinder block walls and bars on the windows. It was one of the most notorious projects in L.A., Imperial Courts. The apartments were scary and a totally different environment from what I was accustomed to. I didn't go outside. My room resembled a jail cell. The sounds of helicopter searches at all hours of the night, gunfire, drug addicts getting high, women selling their bodies were just sounds that eventually put me to sleep many nights. In the daytime, normal was gang-bangers riding by our house with blue bandanas tied around their faces, people in the back of our house smoking PCP and stripping naked as a side effect. This was my new reality. The fear of losing my life daily was real. My heart wondered if I would ever again feel safe and secure.

I am so thankful for the first 14 years of my life. They gave me a foundation on which to dream and build. Deep down I knew that there was more to life than what I saw around me. We didn't come from generational poverty so the lifestyle of many living in Imperial Courts never became my vision. I knew that I could not become a product of my environment. Yes, I lived in the projects but the projects never lived in me. This is when my passion for writing and journaling began.

California Dreaming

As a surrogate teen parent living with four little girls, my teenage life was short-lived. From the break of day, they needed me and I was on duty. My school day started around 5:30a getting myself ready and then getting them off to school. With that accomplished, I started my one-hour commute to Inglewood. My day lasted around sixteen hours. I functioned as their mother in every area of their lives. My weekends were spent ironing all of our clothes for the week, doing hair and washing enormous loads of laundry. I didn't mind helping my mother out. I knew she could not raise four girls without me. I never imagined this responsibility would follow me throughout my entire adult life.

I learned to organize my school life, many family chores, doctor appointments, grocery shopping and helping with all their homework. I barely had time to study myself which made high school difficult and my grades showed it. Keeping up with all I had to do, there was no time to think about what I wanted in life. The only dreams I had were when I slept. I eventually made friends and joined several clubs, which gave me a sense of belonging. I pushed past all the obstacles and diversions placed in my path and managed to graduate. I wasn't at the top of my class, but I finished my course. (Thank You, Lord!)

Swift Transition

I never complained about the work as I reflect; it was extremely taxing mentally and physically. I just honored my mother and loved my nieces. My mother and I were a team. I did what needed to be done. My mother wasn't feeling well most of the time. One week after graduation, she sent me back to Indianapolis to make sure my sister was going to come back to California to care for her children when she was released. I should have known something was wrong. My mother never seemed concerned about my sister's returning before. That summer came and went, and in October I drove my mom to the doctor. It was at the doctor's appointment she was diagnosed with gastric cancer. I had never known anyone with cancer. We went to Sizzler to "celebrate." This might sound odd, but at least she knew what was wrong and why she wasn't feeling well for so long. She never sang a sad song. Once we found out about the cancer, the girls depended on me all the more. Thanksgiving and Christmas came and went, and within twelve weeks of the diagnosis my mother was dead. Two weeks after my mom died, my sister told me I had to go! I was thinking, go where? How could she put me out of my mother's home? The home I helped build for her children? What will happen to my nieces? What was she thinking? I was crushed. I was confounded and confused. I was eighteen, no job and homeless...without my mother or daddy. Looking back, I didn't grasp the seriousness of it all. I felt hurt, rejected and abandoned.

Depressed but Determined

The next several years were spent sleeping in my car under a light post on the corner of Imperial and Crenshaw at Conroy's Flower Shop reading my small Gideon Bible. The words I read in that bible did not make sense to me at the time but were being stored up in me for the days ahead.

I never had the opportunity to properly grieve my mother's death. So much was going on and there was so much to do. I just kept it moving without a thought as to how it was affecting me. Over the course of time clinical depression somehow crept in and took a front row seat in my life. For many years depression hung over my head like a dark rain cloud. No matter where I went it followed. It ruled my life. The choices I made, the agony I felt, and the shame and guilt was overwhelming. I was a vacant shell seeking to be filled. I went places and did things I am too ashamed to mention. I was a walking billboard for guilt and shame. I managed to hide my pain and shame from everyone yet carried the burdens and guilt of others on my shoulders. Depression is not the same for everyone. It creates different problems and has multiple symptoms that affect each person differently. I can remember asking God to just make me normal, just to make me happy and whole.

> *When I began to connect with God's plan of forgiveness and love for me, I was able to completely accept myself just as I was, the same way God accepted me.*

I married. While my marriage was dwindling, I was searching for acceptance, love and validation. The search kept me connected to an additional abusive relationship that lasted for 10 years. I got divorced. One night at the hands of my abuser I was strangled until I was unconsciousness. Another time I was hit in the head so hard until I urinated on myself. I had beer bottles full of liquid cracked across both knees. I've been smacked in the face and even spit on. My self-worth and self-esteem was shot. I began to consume large amounts of alcohol to chase away the hurt and embarrassment of my past choices. Still I was an empty shell longing to be filled. Through all of this there was still something on the inside of me that would not let me give up on life. I couldn't quit. Somehow I had to find the strength to get up and start again.

His Plan, My Purpose

Though broken, misused and abused, God's plan for my life was still working for my good. Of course, I couldn't see it. Each time I made a wrong turn it was His plan that got me back on course. Each time I was knocked down it was His plan that caused me to get back up. Of course, I didn't understand it. His plan was to give me a future, not to harm me but to do me good and bring me to His expected end. I had not reached His expected end so I had to pull myself up, align myself with His plan and start again.

What I realized through all the suffering, pain and disappointment, is that I had to take responsibility for the role I played in where I was in life. If my heart was ever going to be healed and if I was ever going to live a life of value and purpose, I had to do the spiritual, emotional and mental work to overcome.

When I began to connect with God's plan of forgiveness and love for me, I was able to completely accept myself just as I was, the same way God accepted me. It was then and only then that my life began to change significantly. In 2011 while attending a local church, the altar call was given for those who were suffering from depression. It appeared as if the entire congregation walked down the aisle. I was among those that went down. After being prayed for, I was totally delivered from depression. It was like that cloud that followed me around dissipated and I could finally see the warming bright rays of the sun. I received my victory. I was finally free!

I went from a one pound, thirteen-ounce baby girl, sentenced to death to a vibrant successful purpose driven woman full of life! Through almost losing my mind and my life, I have survived that which was supposed to kill me. One day at a time, one step at a time, one victory at a time. I am still here able to share my story with you.

Over 40 years since my uncertain beginning and finally, I DREAM! It has taken over 20 years for me to obtain my undergrad degree, but I did it! There is victory on the other side of depression. There is victory on the other side of rejection. There is victory on the other side of abuse. There is victory on the other side of addiction. There is victory on the other side of every negative thing you have experienced, are experiencing or ever will experience. You just have to hang in there long enough to get to the other side.

Living Life with Deagria

I am still discovering the many gifts that are in me. My passions, gifts, talents are not for me, but are to be used to empower others. I see myself living a rich victorious life. I see you living the same type of life. I see you walking, running, skipping and hopping over obstacles to reach your finish line. You are almost at the finish line! You can't stop now! Your victory is inches away. Stretch! Reach! See it! Feel it! Taste it!

Begin to speak life to yourself! Pour positive words over every negative situation you are facing. Begin to dream again. It does not matter how small or crazy they may seem. Hold on to your dreams. Cultivate and nurture your dreams. Remember, time is of no essence. Do not be hindered by your age or status in life. Connect with power people. Make a conscience effort to live your passion and fulfill your dreams.

Here are thirteen things that God has given me to help me stay the course and be successful in building my dreams. I want to share them with you. I encourage you not to just read them but put them into practice in your life and watch things turn around for you.

1. Find 3 things to LOVE about yourself TODAY
2. Write, write and continue to write
3. Have a gratitude journal... there's plenty of things to be thankful for
4. Embrace and walk in self-care, meditation and prayer
5. Be patient with your journey and give yourself some grace
6. Love and completely accept who you are
7. Cut the cord on guilt, shame and doubt
8. Hold on to your dreams; don't give up
9. You are not your past mistakes
10. Find the good and beauty that's all around you
11. You are meant for a Great purpose
12. You can have the life you desire
13. Walk with a positive attitude; find the good in your circumstances

I have learned the power of forgiveness. I have learned the importance of self-love and self-care. Life and bad circumstances can happen in your life; however, when we seek God, really focus on His love and sacrifice for our lives, we can be victorious.

My desire for you is that you enjoy the journey. Dig deep to the heart of the matter and ask yourself; will this matter five years from now? Be and just do your personal best. As I sit here and write these words I am truly thankful for all the experiences, even the ones I haven't shared with you. Life really has a way of forcing you and me to live out loud. When you are good to yourself life will show up for you.

My prayer for you is that you seek to find the beauty within yourself. I am a survivor of homelessness, domestic violence and crisis living. I encourage you to trust God's plan for your life. Let God speak to you and give you direction. God really can take our dreams to a higher place when we learn to listen to that still voice in our spirit. Always remember to utilize your gifts and talents. Know that you are completely blessed and God really has your best interest at heart. He uses uncomfortable things in our lives to force us to walk in His purpose. Right now you may be uncomfortable in your life, position and even in your own skin. Uncomfortable moments come up to push you to the next level, ultimately creating your authentic self.

Lastly, remember, your story does not have power over you; you have the power to tell your story. Live out your dreams...I believe in you!

Love,

Deagria

Nicole Emery

Nicole Emery is a woman of God, first. She has been married for 15 years to Laman E. Emery Sr. and their son, Laman E. Emery Jr. is 15 years old. Her family is her most treasured gift and are her biggest supporters.

Nicole has been in the medical field for over 18 years as a pharmacy technician. She is a team lead at her current job and works in the Oncology Therapeutic Resource Center where she enjoys helping and serving those on her team and the patients that are going through major storms in their lives.

Nicole has her own business, Abundance of Blessings, where she creates elegant and beautiful gift baskets and centerpieces. She has a bachelor's degree in healthcare administration and business and is currently working towards her MBA in marketing at Indiana Institute of Technology. Nicole is a worshiper and psalmist whose mission is to sing to the nations. She ministers on the praise team at her church and is humbled daily by God's will to use her in every assignment He sends her way. Her daily mission is to love with the heart of Christ, seek God, trust Him, and do His will.

CHAPTER SEVEN

The Training Ground

German philosopher, Friedrich Nietzsche quoted, "Whatever doesn't kill you makes you stronger." God chose me to be a soldier in His army, but I had to be tested and equipped for the work He called me to do.

My training began when I was about five years old when I realized my father wasn't coming home. My parents got divorced when I was four years old. They married each other as teens; she was 15, and my dad was 19. I was born shortly afterwards. At least they tried, I guess, right? One summer day, I sat on the porch with my younger sister, and we waited for my dad to come pick us up for dinner. We wore our pretty dresses; my dress was white with a pink sash, and my sister's was white and powder blue. And the aroma of the grease was in our hair. Our grandmother, who lived next door, used her pressing comb and Marcel curlers to do our hair. Mom wanted us to us look our finest. An hour had passed, and my sister and I were still waiting. Then, the phone rang. My mom came down the stairs and slowly shared the news that our dad wasn't coming to get us. My sister began to cry. Back in those days, I wasn't emotional; I kept everything bottled in. I just went upstairs, hung up my clothes, changed into my regular ones, and starting doing my chores.

A year passes by, and my mom became ill. She didn't know what the issue was. It began with stomach issues — extremely painful flare-ups that kept her in the hospital. In and out of the stomach episodes, my mother would fall into a deep depression, which was later diagnosed as Bipolar disorder. She even attempted suicide a few times. It was a blessing that my grandmother lived next door because we never knew when my mom would be challenged with either the depression or the flare-ups. She took several tests to determine the illness in her stomach, but the doctors were not able to diagnosis her until years later. It was Crohn's disease, a chronic inflammatory disease in the colon that causes excruciating pain.

While she was away, our older cousin would volunteer to watch us. Sometimes, our grandmother had to work or serve at a church function. Our cousin had a nice house and lots of material things, so my sister and I enjoyed visiting. We slept over a few times, and I soon realized why he volunteered to keep us. He was like a leopard moving in to capture his prey. He manipulated those that knew him. He posed himself as a man of God — kindhearted, great with kids, always helpful and selfless. I knew different but never said anything. If my mom found out, she would have literally killed him or slipped into an eternal depression. She was unstable in those days.

The molestation went on for years and not just by him. There was another perpetrator, a distant cousin (by marriage) who visited from the South. He was about five to six years older than me. I fell prey to him as well. It seemed as though I was living three separate lives. The first life was being molested by the older cousin within the closer part of our family. In my second life, I'd come home to the distant cousin that lived directly downstairs from us. He'd ask if I could come down and watch television or play games. Then, there was the third life where I'd go to church every week on Sundays and Wednesdays. Sometimes, I'd go on Fridays and Saturdays, too. I asked God, "Why is this happening to me, I don't understand."

I held everything in; I was so sad, dying on the inside. But on the outside, I tried to appear happy and determined. I masked my pain through grades. I made the honor roll consistently in elementary and middle school. When my mom was home and doing well, she demanded that we make good grades and strived to be successful and independent in life. I couldn't bring home anything less than a "B" on my report card. If I did, she'd flip out. However, she wasn't as strict on my sister about her grades. I didn't think it was fair, but due to the events in my life, did fair even exist? Was there such a thing?

When I was twelve years old, I was diagnosed with a slight case of scoliosis. I had to wear a lift in my shoes to correct the alignment of my spine. Now, there was one more thing I had to deal with. I was already being violated by not one, but two older cousins. I got involved with things at school—different clubs and groups—anything to keep from being at home. On top of that, my mom was in and out of relationships that I did not agree with. And from one of them, another sister was born. This occurred in between the episodes of sickness and depression. I wanted to run away but didn't want to leave my sisters. The only thing I wanted was to run away from the issues that tormented me. When I was 13, the molestation stopped.

Fast forward to my freshman year of high school at age 14. I was so excited because it was a new start. I could put everything else behind me. If I just didn't think about it, it would go away. My mom was feeling better and didn't need someone to help watch us any longer. I came home from school one day and my stomach was aching pretty badly, so I took some Pepto-Bismol. Immediately, it shot right back up; the vomiting was nonstop. After a while, I began to vomit black bile from my belly. That day, my mother rushed me to the emergency room, and I was admitted for several tests. I wouldn't wish that experience upon my worst enemy. The doctors didn't have the medical technology that's available now, so the process was painful and invasive.

After some time, the tests revealed I had ulcerative colitis; I couldn't even pronounce it at first—certainly hadn't heard of it either. It's an inflammatory disease that causes swelling in the large colon. Unlike Crohn's disease that occurs occasionally, my condition was a continuous inflammation in the colon that was combined with chronic diarrhea, rectal bleeding, malnourishment, and severe cramping in the abdomen. I was sicker than sick! The pain in my belly was excruciating! I begged for the Lord to make it go away. The pain was unbearable to the point that I couldn't be still. It seemed that rocking relieved me—made me feel better but only for a few minutes. I was on a NPO (no food by mouth) diet and for a week was solely on intravenous fluids. I wasn't able to keep anything down. Even a liquid diet was difficult to maintain. I wanted to eat so badly but didn't want to begin vomiting again.

While in the hospital, visitors came here and there; they were mainly from church. My mom came daily after work; I knew she was worried. Slowly, I began to feel better, so the doctor put me on soft foods like Jell-O and mashed potatoes. I imagined it was seafood! After some time, I was able to manage a bland diet. My doctor wanted to see if I could keep all my food down, and I did! I was finally released from the hospital on a bland diet and medication. In the meantime, I was upset because I missed quite a bit of school and was behind in my classes. However, I was determined to get an "A" out of every class. I'd remind myself that, "I could do all things through Christ Jesus." Some of my teachers allowed me to make up the missed work, and I was grateful! Looking back, God was showing me His grace, but I wasn't paying much attention.

Two weeks went by and one day, I woke up with a rash that covered my entire body. It looked as though my skin was burned. Also, I had a fever of 104 degrees. My mom immediately went into panic mode, so she and my grandmother rushed me to the hospital. At that point, I was in and out of consciousness. The doctors gave me intravenous fluids with antibiotics, but my body rejected them. That rash affected me externally and internally, yet the emergency room crew didn't have a single clue as to what it was. All they knew was that my temperature was rising, and I was slipping into a coma. I was dehydrated, and the ER doctor was nearly out of options. My mom stepped in the hallway to cry. My pediatric physician walked around the corner and saw her. She explained the situation; then he came in my room. At first sight, he rushed and sent orders to the nurses and ER doctor to have me flown to Riley Children's Hospital in Chicago. There, they discovered that I was stricken with a rare, immune allergic reaction called Steven Johnson's Syndrome. I was allergic to the sulfur in my medication for the ulcerative colitis. My pediatrician had just been reading a book about the illness the night before, and he recognized the symptoms.

Time passed, and I was getting worse. The rash kept spreading which meant I was more susceptible to infection. My lips were swollen, and my tongue was black and hung out of my mouth. I was surrounded by doctors and nurses who tried to keep me alive, yet I was still going in and out of consciousness. The doctors worked diligently to save my life, but they were discouraged as my body rejected the medication. My parents and grandmother were there. Faintly, I heard the doctor say to my mom, "If her body keeps resisting the fluids, she isn't going to make it." My parents cried; I had never seen my dad cry before. I wanted to tell them not to cry, but I was too weak to talk. My grandmother immediately started praying; she cried out to God right there in the emergency room. When she prayed, God commissioned one of his angels to come my way. Soon after that, my vitals increased and my body accepted the medication. I thought my life was ending, but God had other plans for me.

I showed progress but was still in critical care. The rash was getting worse, and my skin was peeling off. That day, I was admitted to Riley Children's Hospital. I had to do daily skin treatments, remain on intravenous fluids, plus maintain the bland diet. One day my mom came to visit me, and I asked her to let me see her mirror. She wouldn't do it at first but finally gave in after I persisted. When I saw myself, I screamed! I was horrified. My tongue and lips were swollen. My skin looked raw, like I had just walked out of a fire. All I could do was cry. I was very vain and conceited back then because I was fair skinned and pretty. My mom tried to console me, but I shut down. Over time, I got better and the sores from the rash began to heal. Christmas Eve had come, and I had begun to feel lonely because I was so far away at Riley Children's Hospital and didn't have many visitors. My mom came to visit, and I asked to her tell my doctor that I didn't want to spend Christmas in the hospital. So he came by for rounds and asked me if I wanted to go home. I screamed with joy! My mom didn't have clothes for me because she didn't expect that I would be discharged, so she took off her clothes and gave them to me. Then, she found some of her boyfriend's work clothes in the trunk of his car, and off we went. I was home on Christmas Day and was so glad. After Christmas break, I went back to school. I was overjoyed at being a normal kid again. I had been in the hospital for almost three months. My body had nearly recovered from the drug reaction; however, I still battled the ulcerative colitis off and on. But now, I had to deal with kids spreading rumors about why I had missed so much school. The rumor was that I had an abortion that didn't go well. Seriously, I wasn't even having sex! All the while, I just kept focused and was determined to pull my grades up. I didn't make the honor roll that semester, but I didn't have any failing grades either. Best of all, I was alive to tell my story.

I am abundantly grateful for how God's love rescued me. I believe He gave me an angel assigned just to me, to be with me through those dark times in my life. This is why I collect ceramic and stone angels today. How beautiful it would have been to have seen my angels' wings overshadowing me that day in the emergency room! I also sing and have been told that my voice is like an angel. It's one of the gifts God gave me. Sometimes, I sing to myself to get through tough moments. I was the worship leader at my former church. Once while ministering, God said, "This is what I have called you to do." God called me to sing, to use my voice as an instrument of praise and a tool to minister compassion, healing, and love. I promised the Lord that I will do His will as He orders my steps.

After the illness, I began to sing in church often. There was one song in particular that many people loved to hear me sing. It's titled, "Order My Steps." My favorite lyrics of the song are "I want to walk worthy, my calling to fulfill. Please order my steps, Lord, and I'll do Your blessed will. The world is ever changing, but You are still the same. If You order my steps, I'll praise Your name." This is what I have been doing each day, praising God and sharing my testimony of how He healed my body through the gift of song.

While on the training grounds of my life, I learned that I must put on my full armor when going through trials. My armor is my praise and trust in God's Word. Ephesians 6:10-17 sums up my training guide. It says, *"Finally, be strong in the Lord and in his mighty power. Put on the full armor of God, so that you can take your stand against the devil's schemes. For our struggle is not against flesh and blood, but against the rulers, against the authorities, against the powers of this dark world and against the spiritual forces of evil in the heavenly realms. Therefore, put on the full armor of God, so that when the day of evil comes, you may be able to stand your ground, and after you have done everything, to stand. Stand firm then, with the belt of truth buckled around your waist, with the breastplate of righteousness in place, and with your feet fitted with the readiness that comes from the gospel of peace. In addition to all this, take up the shield of faith, with which you can extinguish all the flaming arrows of the evil one. Take the helmet of salvation and the sword of the Spirit, which is the word of God."* (NIV)

Another favorite scripture is James 1:2-4 that says, *"Consider it pure joy, my brothers and sisters, whenever you face trials of many kinds, because you know that the testing of your faith produces perseverance. Let perseverance finish its work so that you may be mature and complete, not lacking anything."* (NIV) Today, I live in total healing. My body has been completely restored by God's healing power.

Through the years, I have grown in my walk with the Lord. I have discovered what true freedom is. The Lord told me that, "You must let go of your past and forgive those who have hurt you to be completely free." So I asked Him yet again to lead me and order my steps — to teach me how to forgive. When I was 33 years old,

I asked my older cousin to come talk to me. We were at a family reunion. I'd already forgiven him, but God said, "You need to tell him he is forgiven." When I did, he wept. My cousin said he'd been wanting to apologize but didn't know how. As for the distant cousin, I never saw him again. He moved back to the South, but I forgave him as well. Over the years, my father and I finally developed the relationship that I prayed for. That last chain of bondage had been lifted. Matthew 6:15 says, *"For if you forgive men when they sin against you, your heavenly Father will also forgive you. But if you do not forgive men their sins, your Father will not forgive your sins."* (NIV) Through those years of physical challenge, my mom was always there. I am so grateful that the Lord ceased her illness so that she could stand with me in some of the greatest challenges of my life.

> *My life has not been perfect or fair, but believing in my Lord Jesus Christ, God has restored every part of me. He has led and guided me through each storm. That is His promise; He never leaves, and He always keeps His Word.*

My trials were actually my training ground. I have learned to trust God's Word and listen to His voice. My life has not been perfect or fair, but believing in my Lord Jesus Christ, God has restored every part of me. He has led and guided me through each storm. That is His promise; He never leaves, and He always keeps His Word.

KENNISHA CUNNINGHAM

Kennisha Cunningham was born, raised and resides in Columbus, Ohio and is the second oldest of six siblings. She has been married to her husband, Richard Cunningham Jr for 16 years and is the mother of four children: Gyshelah Jr, Tyrone, Richard III and Yakira. Kennisha also has six grandchildren.

Kennisha attends Rhema Christian Center, pastored by Apostle LaFayette Scales and his wife Theresa, where she is an active volunteer with the Women with Courage ministry. The goal of this ministry is to provide spiritual encouragement and instruction for positive parenting skills for single parent families, something Kennisha is all too familiar with. Kennisha is also currently a student of Unique Women, a two-year course designed after the Majoring in Men curriculum, which was created by the late Edwin Cole to help men understand their roles as Christian men. The course consists of nine books which include titles such as Maximized Manhood and Courage. She is scheduled to graduate with the 2017 class.

Kennisha has earned her bachelors' degrees in Accounting and Forensic Accounting along with attending a myriad of leadership and development courses.

(Continued at conclusion of chapter)

CHAPTER EIGHT

Keep. Moving. Forward. Only Stop at Purpose Complete!

"Hear me, people by the sea. Listen to me, you faraway nations. The LORD called me before I was born. He called my name while I was still in my mother's womb." – Isaiah 49:1 AMP

God created each and every one of us for a specially designed purpose. His thought process was not flawed when He decided that you were meant to be created and living on the earth at this very specific time. God made no mistakes when He fashioned you and mindful thought went into designing the very essence of your being. Even though God formed and fashioned each of us with a desire to fulfill the purpose that He designed for our life, sometimes things happen in our lives that would give the appearance that we have deviated from those predetermined plans. It doesn't change the truth that God wants to witness what He wrote on the tablet for your life to come to pass. According to Romans 8:28 in the amplified version, "That's why we can be so sure that every detail in our lives of love for God is worked into something good." In the paragraphs fol-

MY STORY. GOD'S GLORY.

lowing, you will have the opportunity to take a peek into my life as I share with you My Story...God's Glory.

My Story...

As a little girl, I loved to read all the time. I would check out several books from the library and just lay in bed every day reading. I would read magazines, newspapers or anything that I could get my hands on. I dreamt of going off to college and getting my degree. I desired to travel the world and learn about different cultures and understand how people of other ethnic backgrounds lived. I just knew that eventually one day I would get married and have two children – a boy and a girl (in that order). Overall, I envisioned becoming a well-rounded, well-educated, well-paid, successful person living the good life. But, things didn't quite turn out as I planned.

One thing you have to understand is that as a little girl, my daddy was my world. I did everything with him. I remember when we would study the bible as a family. We would gather around the dining room table and have discussions about the different people in the bible. I remember a time when my dad quizzed us on how to pronounce the word 'reality' during one of our study sessions. Although, I knew that I knew how to pronounce the word, I nor my siblings could quite get it out correctly! When my dad revealed to us how to pronounce the word properly, we all just laughed and kind of beat ourselves up because none of us could pronounce it right.

Another memory I have of my daddy was when he would work on his cars. I would be right out there with him, looking over the engine and asking him what each part of it was and what it was used for. When it was time to change a tire, I remember asking my dad what each part of the tire was, from the spokes to the lug nuts on down to the crowbar used to remove the tire. I remember being under the hood with my daddy as he would show me what the carburetor was and how to look at it to tell if it was still working properly. Oil changes were also fun because we would actually slide under the car and look at how to drain the oil from the ground up.

One of the fondest memories of them all is when we planted a garden in a section of our backyard. We would go to the store and my parents would pick out which seeds they wanted to plant in the garden. I used to help out with the actual planting of the seeds by taking a hoe and breaking up the soil to prepare the dirt. We planted seeds for foods such as green beans, greens, watermelon and corn. A season after the seeds were planted, we would always check for the first signs of growth: a stem, a leaf or some sort of sprout that gave an indication that the seeds we planted were going to produce a harvest. For instance, we would watch for that ear of corn to grow forth from the stalk. And when it appeared to be ready, we would pull an ear of corn from the stalk, shuck it and check it to see if the ear was full of corn and if the corn was a deeper yellow in color. If not, we knew that it wasn't quite time to harvest all of the corn. A little while later, we would pull another ear of corn and check again to see if the corn was ready to be harvested. If so, we would take buckets to pull each of the ears of corn that were ready from the stalks. We also planted little hand sized watermelons and they would grow out from the vine with such a pretty green color. Once the watermelon had grown to maturity, I pulled one of them off of the vine and opened it. Inside was a deep red color. Eating the watermelon was the fun part. It was so small, yet so sweet.

Harvesting our produce was a joy for our family. It meant that we had sown good seed into good soil and that the seed received the proper care and nutrition by way of receiving water and was protected from any potential predators that would destroy the crop. And finally, it meant that we gathered the crops at the right time – not too soon or it wouldn't be ripe but also not too late that the crops had spoiled prior to being harvested.

So, life was great and was flowing quite nicely in my life as a little girl. I made good grades in school and honor roll was a frequent achievement for me. But mind you, we didn't have much. At least not according to what others defined as having much. My daddy was the sole financial provider while my mother cared for the children and the household. You would never be able to tell six children lived in our home. My mother kept our home "spic and span" clean. So much so, you could just about eat off the floors! The family would be notified of breakfast and dinner by a pretty white gold-trimmed glass bell my mom rang when it was time to eat. We ate off of gold trimmed china and shiny, polished silverware at our family sized dinette table, set with fancy place settings, and matching china cabinet. We drank out of crystal stemware. We would pull our cloth napkins from the ring and place it in our lap after our father blessed the food. As far as I was concerned, we were royalty and had the world: a nice home, a family with a mother and a father, siblings to play with, clothes on our back, food on the table and multiple vehicles to transport our large family wherever we wanted to go. Who could ask for more? There was no stopping this little girl and I was well on my way to becoming everything I had dreamed of. That is, until one day, my life took a drastic turn.

At the young age of 11, the dynamics of my family changed. One night when my dad got home, he was met by the police and escorted from our family home. Then the unexpected happened. My parents were getting divorced! This had a tremendous impact on my life as my daddy, my rock, my very foundation was leaving our family home, for good. Never to return. What was a little daddy's girl supposed to do? Who was going to teach me things going forward? As a result, my world was turned upside down. There was a void that I did not understand how to fill. Ultimately, I became a teenage mother at the age of 14. FOUR-

TEEN! Can it get any worse? It did. I became a mother for a second time at the age of 15. Whoa! What? Two children by the age of 15?! What was a young mother to do? How could I possibly be successful in life and fulfill all of my dreams when I already had two kids with no high school education?

God's Glory...

"For I know the thoughts that I think toward you, saith the LORD, thoughts of peace, and not of evil, to give you an expected end. 12 Then shall ye call upon me, and ye shall go and pray unto me, and I will hearken unto you." Jeremiah 29:11-12 KJV

Still in high school, I vowed that I was not going to remain, what I called, a 'negative statistic.' I made a vow to myself that I was not going to live my life on public assistance. I was determined to graduate, on time and with my original graduating class and still lead a productive life. But how?

I am here to tell you...but GOD! I didn't quite understand it all at the time. And some of it is still unclear to me today. But when I look back over the years, I realize that God was, and still is, working out His purpose and His plan for my life. You see, back in high school while in the ninth grade, I was given the opportunity to work with a tutor to complete my high school coursework of the main subjects while I was out of school after delivering my child. This was such a blessing because when I returned to high school, I picked up with the rest of the class as if I had been there the whole time. This was only the beginning of my journey. Not only did I graduate on time with my class, I graduated with the college preparatory bar on my high school diploma! You see, earning that college preparatory bar on my diploma meant that I took a number of courses in high school that would prepare me for going to college. And I did just that!

I started out by attending our local community college.

I made the Dean's List several times during the course of my studies. I ultimately graduated with an associate's degree which also earned me the honor of being the first person in my family to earn a college degree. I was also able to become gainfully employed while going to school. I got married and the most important decision I ever made in my life was giving my life to God. My husband and I were both saved on the same date and were also baptized at the same time. Thirteen years after having my second child, I gave birth to my third child. Four years after that, I had my fourth child. And would you believe that after the birth of my fourth child, I returned to one of our local universities and earned not one, but two bachelor's degrees?! Not too bad for a little daddy's girl turned teenage mother of two by the time she was fifteen, huh?

> *God made no mistakes when He fashioned you and mindful thought went into designing the very essence of your being.*

Now, don't get me wrong. It wasn't necessarily easy to accomplish all that I have accomplished to date. There were a lot of obstacles I faced during the course of this time. There were many times I wondered what God wanted to do with this life of a former teenage mother. Even after obtaining two bachelor's degrees would you believe I still didn't think it was enough? In actuality, it wasn't. God has so much more in store for me. And I do not believe God allowed me to go through all that I went through for no reason. I believe that God wants to use my life as an example to other teenage parents to let them know that it is not the end of the world simply because you became a teenage parent. You can still fulfill the purpose God has for your life and be successful in spite of the fact of becoming a teenage parent.

Just as my daddy and I planted seeds in our backyard garden and expected to receive a harvest from the seeds that were sown, God has given me this opportunity to tell my story to plant the seed in you to let you know that God is not through with you yet! He expects to receive a harvest from the seed of purpose that He has placed within you. You see, God placed you in your mother's womb and you were born for this very moment and time to fulfill a specified purpose. God has an expectation that what He has purposed to produce through and by your very life will be manifested in reality. God desires to use your testimony to encourage others to put their faith and trust in Him and to know that no matter what you experience, He has a purpose and a plan for your life.

The exciting news is that God is not done with me yet. And if you are reading this testimony of how I was able to overcome the obstacles of being a teenage mother to get to where I am today, please know that God is not done with you yet either. It is God's desire to see what He has said about you since before the foundations of the world come to pass. Don't give up on yourself and most certainly don't give up on God. Even if you are not 100% clear about the purpose and call that God has on your life, keep moving forward! If you've had a child as a young teenager, or even if some other happenstance occurred in your life: drugs, alcohol, prostitution, or some other downfall, it doesn't matter; **do not** believe the lie that there is no purpose for your life! How do you know you have purpose? Because you are here! God absolutely has plans for you to get you to His expected end. There is nothing that you or anyone else can do to cancel out, negate or refute the purpose that God has preordained for you to fulfill. "For the gifts and calling of God are without repentance." Romans 11:29a KJV. So go and do all that God places in your heart to do!

One very important point that I am compelled to make is that in order to fully understand the purpose God has for you is that you have to give your life to God and allow the Holy Spirit to come into your heart so that He can lead you down the pathway that you are meant to go. This is called "being born again." It is vital for you to be able to hear the voice of the Lord through the Holy Spirit so that you can communicate with God to discover what your purpose is. God will provide you with detailed information and instructions to fulfill your purpose, but that cannot happen if you have never accepted Jesus into your life as your personal Lord and Savior. If you have never accepted Jesus into your life, do not fret. Today is your day! If you believe on Jesus, the prayer of salvation is ready for you to confess and a sample prayer has been provided for you below. Are you ready to accept Jesus as your personal Lord and Savior? If the answer is 'Yes," then say this prayer with me:

Prayer of Salvation...

God in heaven, I confess that I am a sinner who needs a savior. I thank you Lord that you loved me enough to redeem my life from destruction. I believe that Jesus died on the cross, shed His blood for my sins and arose again that I may live. I ask you Lord to forgive me of all my sins. I accept Jesus as Lord and Savior into my life. Search my heart and I ask you to cleanse me of all unrighteousness. Help me Lord to know you in an intimate way so that I may walk upright in your sight. Thank you God for saving me this day from the grips of death and allowing me to receive my new life in you. In Jesus name I pray. Amen.

Now rejoice! Hallelujah! God has now taken up residence within you and the power you need to prevail in life is alive and living on the inside of you. His name is Holy Spirit and He will help guide you into your destiny. I pray that you ask God to lead you to a local, word-based church where you can receive more in-depth biblical teachings to help you continue on your love walk, on to ultimately fulfilling your purpose. If you have prayed this prayer, I'm very excited about your new life in Christ and would love to hear all about it! You can contact me via email at *kennishacunningham@yahoo.com.*

In closing, please be reminded of this: God loves you. He wants only the very best for you. What greater gift to give the Lord than to walk in the purpose that He has called you to? God predestined you for greatness. We are victorious in Him. When we place our trust and our confidence in Him, He will order our steps to get us to His expected end. Not *our* expected end, but *His* expected end. Whatever the calling is in your life and no matter what obstacles you may face in this life, always keep this in the forefront of your mind: Keep. Moving. Forward and Only Stop at Purpose Complete!

Endnotes:
Isaiah 40:31 KJV
Isaiah 49:1 AMP
Romans 8:28 AMP
Jeremiah 29:11-12 KJV
Romans 11:29a KJV

BIOGRAPHY CONTINUED

One of her favorite scriptures is Isaiah 40:31 KJV:
"But they that wait upon the LORD shall renew their strength; they shall mount up with wings as eagles; they shall run, and not be weary; and they shall walk, and not faint."

To Kennisha, this scripture serves as a constant reminder of how we as Christians are to be as it pertains to fulfilling our purpose.

Latonia Price

I'm Latonia Price, a certified life coach, author and aspiring public speaker. I've been married to Elder Iradel Price for over 7 years. I currently live in Indianapolis, Indiana. I am the youngest of four siblings - three sisters and one brother.

I base my coaching on Biblical principles and am blessed to be an active member of Puritan Missionary Baptist Church. I truly love God and strive to live a life holy and acceptable to Him. My mission is to help people live life more effectively through solution-focused, transformational coaching methods and techniques.

My vision is to effectively empower, encourage, and motivate individuals to tell their story (testify) and positively move forward in fulfilling their God-given destiny!

I love to learn! I have a Bachelor of Science in Computer Information Technology and two Master degrees in Computer Information Systems. I also love to read and do things that allows me to be creative, e.g. cooking, writing, graphic design, hair styling, etc. In the coming years, I would love to partake in more ministry opportunities that allow me to utilize my creativity. Along with my coaching certifications, I also received another certification in December 2015 through Authentic Identity Institute: Certified Human Behavior Consultant (CHBC). I am the author of several books. They are all available through my website, *www.effectiveliving-llc.com,* and through Amazon.com.

In the coming years, I desire to write more books and speak to those around the world about how faith in God is truly the path to a better life.

CHAPTER NINE

My 'Shaking' for the Greatest Glory

"...In a little while I will once more shake the heavens and the earth, the sea and the dry land. I will shake all nations, and what is desired by all nations will come, and I will fill this house with glory...The glory of this present house will be greater than the glory of the former house,' says the Lord Almighty..." (Hag. 2:6-7, 9 NIV)

I believe that when a child is born into this world, the heavens rejoice! It's another soul that God has purposed and destined for greater works than the previous generations. Although the soul is wrapped in flesh and birthed into a sinful world, the hopes and future are already marked with a promise of God's marvelous manifestations. As the child grows and matures, sin is soon discovered, and now another birthing process must begin. This birthing process is a spiritual journey of reconnecting, establishing, and maintaining the original relationship with the Creator. Sometime during this spiritual birthing process God has to allow some 'shaking' to occur.

The Preparation: The Greater Glory

When I was young, I had no deep understanding about Christianity. My parents taught me the foundational truths about God and Jesus Christ. They bought me the adorable Bible story books because I loved to read and soon they became a part of my library. I didn't come to an understanding about Christianity until God initiated my spiritual birthing process. He had to cause a 'shaking' of my foundation about what I knew and read as a child. This 'shaking' began when I was four-teen years old and was diagnosed with cancer. The process was frightening and overwhelming because I was still a child who didn't know much about life. At that point, I had just begun to understand the basics of life and was learning how to use, what the older gen-eration calls, common sense. The 'shaking' at the age of 14 that God allowed, helped me to recognize what my strengths are because he knew what my hopes for the future were.[1] He had to take me through a preparation process to obtain the greater glory.

After my cancer treatments and recovery, God al-lowed me to continue living. I had a greater apprecia-tion for life and made a vow to thank Him every day for everything! I soon joined a local church ministry and got involved with different groups within the church. This helped me move further in my spiritual birthing journey. I fed on the milk[2] of God's word and gained strength to further desire the meat that God wanted me to eat. I soon began to attend more conferences and discovered the importance of my personal relationship with God. I learned the importance of striving to live a life that is holy and acceptable to God because this was a part of my true service[3] in the Kingdom of God. I didn't make all the right decisions as I started to be-come a young adult but God yet kept me safe and cov-ered during my maturing process.

I had other times when God had to 'shake' the foun-dations during my spiritual maturing process.

Once I passed the birthing process, God knew I would need other series of 'shaking' because God needed it for his glory to be even greater! I endured two car accidents that I should not have survived. Inappropriate friendships and immature relationships caused me to lack confidence in myself and in my worth. I was trying to sacrifice for others while thinking I could still sacrifice for God. These relationships and friendships caused self-inflicted emotional issues. I made the decision to do these acts that were not pleasing to God. After surviving the car accidents and overcoming those self-inflicted emotional issues, I became more aware, and strived harder to do more for God.

The Spiritual Growth: Full of Greater Glory

Soon I obtained my college degree. I was working diligently with another local church ministry and striving to be more obedient to God's will. As I was more focused on Christian ministry, I was soon found by my husband. We spent time together during our courtship, which allowed us to mature even more in God, and really learn more about what God ordained for our lives. After our three-year courtship, we made the vow before God in holy matrimony. We had a wonderful celebration and God blessed us with exceeding abundance from the very beginning.

After a few years of marriage, we began to desire a family. We started to plan and take action to conceive a child. After the first year and a half of not conceiving, we decided to consult our family doctor. I became very afraid because I knew my medical history. I felt that I was at fault for not conceiving since I was the one who had cancer and chemotherapy at the age of 14. Soon our doctor began to run tests and we had appointments with fertility specialists. After conducting even more extensive and painful tests, all proved to be sufficient for conception. The fertility doctor did prescribe special medication to help us to continue trying. After the very first month of being on the special medication, we conceived our first child!

After all the tests and emotions of conceiving, we felt God's glory was great in that season! We felt we had witnessed a mighty and awesome manifestation of one his promises for our lives. We were filled with joy and great expectations of becoming parents to a healthy, beautiful baby girl! We named her Charlotte Evelina. It was a combination of my grandmother (Charlotte) and my husband's mother (Evelina).

We celebrated and rejoiced throughout the pregnancy process. We had the normal events and made purchases in preparation for the arrival of Charlotte Evelina. We got all the baby furniture, clothes, toys, feeding supplies, etc. We did what normal expecting parents do! Our families were so happy for us and were becoming just as anxious as time drew closer to her arrival. However, unknown to us, God had other plans for another 'shaking.'

The Strongest 'Shaking' Ever

The week before our daughter was due to arrive, I felt very uneasy about the latest prenatal visit. Our OB/GYN had a difficult time finding the heartbeat but once the heartbeat was discovered, we left the office as normal. However, I didn't feel her movements like I had before. I ignored it based on the fact of what nurses say, once you are in the final weeks of pregnancy – the baby won't have much room to move so the movements aren't felt as much. The next morning, I was still worried because there was no movement for the first few hours. I called the office and scheduled a same day stress test. I arrived for the appointment and they performed the normal task of hooking up the monitors for the stress test. The nurse had a difficult time locating the heartbeat so she had another nurse try. Then I was taken to an exam room and a doctor tried to find the heartbeat. Still no heartbeat. Finally, I was in an ultrasound room with the doctor and nurse. As they passed the small instrument across my jelly-covered belly, I looked up at the black and white image on the small monitor. I didn't see much of anything and I didn't hear anything either. I just hoped maybe the volume was low or turned off. Sadly, it was not. The doctor walked over to the other side of the exam bed and grabbed my hand to announce Charlotte Evelina was no longer alive. I was numb. Then I began to cry harder than I've ever cried before. My body began to shake. God literally gave me one of the most devastating 'shaking' events I had ever encountered!

The next several hours were like a slow motion picture. My worst nightmare had occurred; it was like a tragic horror movie was showing with me in the leading role. The only exception was that this wasn't a fictional event. My labor was induced and I was giving birth to Charlotte's lifeless body. Despite the stale quietness of the room, I was able to see her and hold her. She was beautiful! Thick black hair, long eyelashes, big cheeks, and she had my skinny fingers. Her features were actually a combination of both her grandmother and great-grandmother! She was simply gorgeous!

As the hours and days went by, it was time to leave the hospital. In those couple of days, I had stopped feeling numb and completely sad. I didn't really feel anything until I made my way downstairs to the hospital exit. As I waited for our car to be pulled around, I suddenly become overwhelmed with so many emotions. I watched the other mothers and fathers carrying car seats with their newborns. They looked so excited and happy! Some even had pink or blue balloons to showcase the celebration. However, I had no car seat or balloons. I had a bag of dirty clothes and other small tangible keepsakes of my stillborn child. As I arrived home, every emotion that could possibly be imagined began to surface. The strongest of those was anger towards God's will!

As we made the funeral arrangements, we had to think about the life of Charlotte Evelina. Even though she only lived for 9 months within me, my husband and I were able to recall different aspects of Charlotte's life and characteristics. She loved pineapple since anytime I would eat them, she would move a lot. I even remember when I scheduled the 3D ultrasound appointment the nurse had said to eat 30 minutes before the appointment. This will help the baby to be awake during the ultrasound. I ate pineapple, and sure enough, she was moving! In fact, she gave the biggest smile that I ever witnessed on a baby inside the womb. She was happy and safe! She was warm and healthy! She didn't have to endure the evils of this world. Her life was perfect!

Although we were able to reminisce about this and give some words about her life for the funeral program, it still didn't make the anger, frustration, fear, sadness, loneliness, emptiness, depression, and all those other overwhelming emotions go away. I still wasn't sure why God had to select us and that season to 'shake' our earth and land. I wasn't ready to accept the greater glory!

After facing previous trials and obstacles (the other 'shaking' occurrences), I understood the greater glory that God desired for our lives. However, I wasn't ready; I just wanted our baby! I thought of her being alive and raising her was the greater glory God ordained. Not being ready caused me to not trust God with my deepest desires. If that was his plans for obtaining greater glory, I didn't want any part of it! I soon stopped asking God for anything except for the basic needs, e.g. food, shelter, health, strength to work and drive, etc. However, God knew this wouldn't last long; he still needed to fill me with an even greater glory!

The Recovery: The Greatest Glory

I stopped having intimate talks with God; I started not having intimate talks with my husband. I was having panic attacks at work. I was feeling the physical side effects of these overwhelming emotions; constantly sleeping, dizziness, headaches, chest pains, etc. My life was not going back to the normal state that it was before and during the pregnancy. My husband soon had to give me one of the longest and deepest talks he had ever given me. I cried while he talked to me and I cried for a couple days afterward. I soon wanted something that I knew would only come from one source: God. I wanted to be made whole again! I wanted to be filled with the greatest glory I would experience in my life. It had to be even greater than before in order to destroy all those overwhelming and negative emotions in my mind!

Soon I was reading the Bible to find some encouragement and empowerment. After a few failed attempts, I did find some stories that helped to empower and encourage me. The stories of Hannah[4] and the woman with the issue of blood[5] helped me to recognize some important facts of faith. They both had unrelenting faith because they kept seeking God for their deepest desire. Hannah wanted a child, after so many years of not conceiving and being tormented by watching other women birthing children who her husband fathered. The woman with the issue of blood got all the medical attention possible, which left her broken physically and mentally. Despite all of this, they both decided to keep trying and seeking God until they got to that one final attempt that unlocked their miracle! They didn't care who saw them or if they had to press their way through a large crowd. It didn't matter to them when it happened, they just knew if they kept seeking and asking, they'd eventually get their breakthrough. Eventually, both women received their miracles and breakthroughs. Both gave God praise when it happened. Their faith made them whole! I needed faith to make me whole!

One night, I was alone at home while my husband was at work. As I finished reading the Bible, I decided to finally have some intimate prayer time with God. I laid a bed sheet down on the floor and grabbed my bottle of blessed oil. I proceeded to lie on the bed sheet, on the floor, and soon I just started telling God, 'Thank you.' After so many weeks, I really didn't know where to begin but with that. I just kept repeating those two words with a sincere heart. Then a shift happened and the spirit of God fell on me. I cried for what seemed like hours as I just poured my all out to God. I was honest with God about I how I felt, how I missed Charlotte, how I wanted my marriage to be better again, and how I wanted to be made whole again! As I was pouring out, God was filling me with the greatest glory, I began to feel the strongholds being released. He began to speak to me, allowing peace to overtake me. That night marked the beginning of the rebuilding process after the strongest 'shaking' of my life.

Being Filled with the Greatest Glory

Day by day, I became spiritually stronger. The overwhelming emotions were starting to fade. I was able to change out my spirit of heaviness into my garment of praise.6 I called that changing my clothes in the dark season! I soon was able to talk and rebuild intimacy with my husband. I was no longer having panic attacks at work. The smile I had was genuine and no longer a fake mask to avoid conversations. I truly was being made whole and being filled with the greatest glory I ever had!

Often times God will allow some 'shaking' to take place in our lives! Each time this happens, God is trying to break up and tear down the weaknesses that are keeping us bound. In Haggai 1-2, the people of God were in the process of rebuilding the temple again. Many of the older people were speaking about how the other temple was and they sort of reminisced about the different features which discouraged the people who were building.

> *It is difficult to stand during God's 'shaking' experiences. In fact, it can seem like the very ground you are walking on, your ideal foundation of faith, disappears.*

They were working hard to make the temple just as great. However, God had to speak through his prophet Haggai and explain that the process of the 'shaking' and the greater glory that was to come. He had to explain that even though the previous temple had all this silver, gold and other great features, this present temple that was being built, was about to be filled with something more valuable than any worldly possession! The tabernacles and altars of the Old Testament could only be filled or covered by a cloud to represent God's presence. Although most of these were dedicated to God, soon other kinds of altars and items were made that were not, which caused idolatry to occur.

God had to allow some 'shaking' of the heavens and earth to happen in order to tear down those altars of idolatry. Soon more 'shaking' of the heavens and earth were to occur because Jesus Christ was coming! He would be coming into that same temple they were building to teach, preach, and save those who were lost. He would heal the sick and raise the dead! Once he died, there was an even stronger 'shaking' of the heavens and earth that caused the veil in the temple to be torn! Now, we are the temples and can be filled with his presence which is also the greater glory!

It is difficult to stand during God's 'shaking' experiences. In fact, it can seem like the very ground you are walking on, your ideal foundation of faith, disappears. The trust level that once was there decreases so quickly and drastically that you ultimately are so speechless that you don't say anything to God. However, I am a witness that it is possible to remain standing and regain your trust in God again! I am a witness that God will make you whole and restore all that you have lost! God wants and needs his glory to be seen! This may require a stronger 'shaking' but that ultimately means he has the greatest glory in store for your life! As you continue to walk with God and be filled with his glory, know that each time you come out of a storm you will be filled with his glory! You will be stronger and greater than before – eventually leading to a level of extraordinary glory and beyond!

End Notes

1 – NIV, Jeremiah 29:11

2 – NIV, 1 Peter 2:2

3 – NIV, Romans 12:1

4 – NIV, 1 Samuel 1

5 – NIV, Mark 5:25-34

6 – NIV, Isaiah 61:3

Le Angela Hardiman

Born and raised in Indianapolis Indiana, Le Angela graduated from Lawrence North High school and IUPUI. Le Angela is the proud mother of a very active 15-year-old son.

She is passionate about writing and is an aspiring playwright. Now, a published author, Le Angela is seizing this opportunity to follow her dream. Her motto in life is to follow your dream and live life to the fullest. She is determined not to let the struggles of her past be in vain. Beginning with her son to the stranger on the street, Le Angela inspires others to be great from the inside out. That is true success!

CHAPTER TEN

Transformed

Be ye transformed by the renewing of your mind. (KJV, Romans 12:2)

Tired! Stressed! Overweight! Sick and tired of being sick and tired. Past due not only on the rent but also on life, I knew just how I desired and dreamed my life should be; how to attain it was the problem. In my subconscious, I probably thought I didn't deserve it. Because I didn't deserve it, I always put myself last on the list and was constantly overwhelmed by issues of my past, childhood trauma, rejection and failed relationships. Suppressing every hurtful experience was my survival mechanism. My outward appearance gave the illusion I was okay, when in reality, I was dying a slow death, decaying from the inside out. It was only a matter of time before I collapsed from the pain and my secrets were revealed. I needed help, a divine intervention. It was time for me to face the past that was keeping me stagnated and motionless. If I didn't, I would die right where I was.

The Past

"Only by acceptance of the past can you alter it." – T.S. Eliot

I remember as if it were yesterday. It was a cool

and gloomy day as if it might rain. As I looked out of the window, I waited for my aunt to come and pick me up. Today was the day and my stomach was in knots; it felt like I would be sick. I can't do this! How come no one asked me what I wanted? My aunt arrived, and we made the journey of what seemed like the longest car ride ever from Indianapolis, Indiana to Plainfield, Indiana. My nine-year-old mind didn't know how to express what I was feeling, so I remained silent, but it felt as if a storm was raging on the inside of me. Conflicting emotions and fear, I wanted to be rescued from what I did not understand. There it is a big brick building; we walk in and my aunt signs us in. Guards greet us and instruct us to remove our shoes and proceed to pat us down. Now, we are told to walk through a metal detector and two doors before entering a room with lots of chairs and people visiting with their family and loved ones. We sit down. After a few minutes, I look up and there he is standing right in front of me, my father. He was put in jail when I was a baby so I didn't know him. I had only seen pictures of him and heard stories about him. Now here he is. I wasn't even sure what to call him. This is a lot for a nine-year-old to comprehend. It was frightening to meet my father for the first time under these circumstances. This was the first of many visits over the next five years and I never got used to it. He passed away a few years later when I was 14 years old.

Fairy Tales

Just about every little girl has a fairy tale. I think we are conditioned to believe that a prince will come along and rescue us. It is a part of our gender roles as boys play with trucks and action figures and are taught to be tough and little girls play with dolls and doll houses and fantasize about being a princess. The death of my father made me very aware that fairy tales don't exist. Fantasies about him coming to rescue me, providing the emotional stability I needed, the love I lacked, and him making me feel complete, formed how I viewed life. He was the hero that would rescue me from my reality. The realities that my home life made me feel invisible and all alone. Growing up with my mom and two older siblings there was such a huge age difference we never talked or had much interaction; the relationship between us was toxic. My heart yearned to feel loved and supported. I know that my mom did the best she could to raise three kids alone. Maya Angelou said, "You did then what you knew how to do, and when you knew better, you did better." My soul (mind, will, emotions) was dying, and I needed to know that I mattered. In my 14-year-old mind I somehow believed that my father would make everything right; he was the answer to my prayers. When he passed away, I was devastated and heartbroken realizing my dream of wanting a father in my life would never come true. I fell into a deep depression not long after that; I felt hopeless. Sleep and tears were a big part of my teenage years. The struggles of depression, trying to make myself feel like I mattered and wondering if anyone at all loved me, sent me searching in all the wrong places. Needing to dull the pain of feeling unloved, the desire for affection, and the need to be touched led me into a promiscuous lifestyle. I went from one broken relationship to another.

At 16 I was a typical teenager hanging out with my friends at the mall and after the mall we would go to an under 21 club. I enjoyed dancing and partying, but I always had to find a ride home so I could be home before church on Sunday morning. It never mattered how I got home, just as long as I did. On this one particular night there was a guy at the club I had hung out with a few times before. I had seen him at the mall but I didn't personally know him. He had a car and offered to take me home. Being young and naïve, I accepted his offer. About ten minutes into the drive it was apparent he was not taking me home; we ended up at a park; I was clueless. Did he think I was going to have sex with him even after I told him NO!!? He forced himself on me and raped me. I was afraid, and I didn't fight back. Afterwards, he took me home, and I felt awful! Why didn't I fight? I got out of the car… went into the house… straight to the bathroom. How ironic this happened just down the street from where my father had committed the same crime! My father was in prison because he raped and killed a woman. I was ashamed and for the first time angry at my father. The realization sunk in. How could he do something so demoralizing to someone else's daughter having one of his own? How could he have truly loved me? I opened the medicine cabinet, and I took whatever was there. It was my first suicide attempt, but not the last. I don't think I wanted to die. I wanted the pain to go away; I wanted to forget everything I had been thru and I didn't know how to cope or deal with the pain and shame of my past so I suppressed it.

Broken

For I know the plans I have for you, "declares the Lord, "plans to prosper you and not to harm you, plans to give you hope and a future. (KJV, Jeremiah 29:11)

My downward spiral with depression continued into adulthood. I was addicted to unhealthy relationships. The insatiable need for feeling loved, wanting to be hugged and held kept me bound in relationships that were detrimental to my well-being. The addiction overpowered my true need, genuine unconditional love. I desired healthy loving relationships but I could only attract what I was intimate with, rejection and hurt. I was a magnet for men that were not willing to love, honor or respect me. My background was so negative I didn't know how to be happy. Peace and joy eluded me. I knew I needed a change I was tired of just existing. I wanted to live!

At twenty-one I had my son. I wanted to be the best mom I could be, but how could I do that when I wasn't even being the best me I could be? My career consisted of moving from one job to the next, never challenging myself or allowing others to challenge me to do or be better. I never had much confidence in myself or my abilities and saw no reason why anyone else should either. Mediocrity caused me to fail at almost everything. My view of myself was damaging not only to me but also to others. I often wondered why negativity surrounded me. Why could I not succeed?

My last suicide attempt was when I was about thirty-five; I was so tired of everything, felt hopelessly depleted in my emotions and spirit! God had placed dreams and ideas in my heart, but I didn't know how to fulfill them. Ideas for being an entrepreneur, writing plays, book ideas, just to name a few, were present. I didn't know where to start. That frustrated me. There was so much vision in me that it was getting hard to function at my regular 9 to 5 job. That upset me. I wasn't living my dream; I asked God why did you make me this way; why did you place these things in my heart? How come I can't be satisfied with going to work every day? Past failure, negative thinking, low self-esteem, depression and heartache was all I knew. Looking back kept me from seeing forward where my dreams were waiting. I was a statistic and that was no longer acceptable! I medicated myself with Vicodin and washed it down with vodka. Thankfully, this attempt also failed. The hardest part to waking up after trying to kill myself was the realization that I am still alive and I don't know why. "God, why did you spare me?" Then I realized I had to deal with everything I suppressed for so long, everything hidden. It was time to get to the root of my problem and it was up to me. I had to choose to get things back on track and that was scary. I walked around oppressed and depressed for months. I remember praying time and time again, "Lord please do not allow what I have gone thru to be in vain; please allow it to help someone else." I prayed that prayer so many times. *"All things work together for good for those who love God & are called according to his purpose"* (KJV, Romans 8:28). Just like the scripture said, I wanted it to work out for my good.

The Awakening

Every great dream begins with a dreamer. Always remember, you have within you the strength, the patience, and the passion to reach for the stars to change the world. ~Harriet Tubman

One day just out of the blue, I had an "awakening," a light bulb moment, an intervention or whatever you want to call it. It was at this point in my life I realized I was not getting any younger and the only person keeping me from my dreams was me. If I wanted to accomplish God's plan for my life, I had to stop allowing my past to imprison me and keep me in bondage. Fear of failing could no longer be a crutch for not moving forward. In fact, I nicknamed myself "FearlessLe." The remainder of 2015 and into 2016 was going to be spent taking down my fears one at a time and living my life to the fullest. I was determined to tackle my goals and challenge myself, no matter how afraid I was. This was no longer just about me. My life was not even my own. So, who was I to not share my gifts and talents because I was afraid? I like to listen to Joyce Meyer and something she would say resonated with me, "When you are afraid to do something, do it afraid!" I knew that is what I had to do. So begins my journey.

New Beginnings, (The Re-invention of a single mom)

I am not a product of my circumstances. I am a product of my decisions. –Stephen Covey

The first thing I needed to do to get my life in order was to be real with myself by telling myself the truth. Although it was my circumstances that broke me, it was my decisions that were holding me back. If I continued along this same path, it would destroy my destiny. Being honest with myself gave me clarity. My purpose, what I wanted for my life and the legacy I wanted to leave for my son were laid out before me. One of the first things I had to do was change my thinking. I listened to inspirational messages and surrounded myself with positive people. I would listen to Les Brown, Eric Thomas, Joyce Meyer, and Lisa Nichols every day. I listened to people who had been where I had been and were already succeeding at what I wanted to do. Those messages allowed me to know that even though I wasn't where I wanted to be, I knew that it was possible.

> *If I wanted to accomplish God's plan for my life, I had to stop allowing my past to imprison me and keep me in bondage.*

After I changed my thinking, the next step was to change my language and the things I was saying about myself and my future. The Bible says in Romans 4:17 that Abraham believed in God, who gave life to dead things and called into existence the things that did not exist. I believed in the same God so I started speaking what He spoke. I typed out affirmations that were personal, read them out loud always in present tense (calling those things that do not exist into existence). When I said, "I will be successful" I was calling success to me. I would say things like, "I am the lender and not the borrower; prosperity of every kind is drawn to me; everything I touch is a success."

Even though my past was negative, as a child, I always pictured myself doing what I wanted to do. I was always a dreamer; picturing myself speaking and encouraging others, being an author and being very successful. It was vision that gave me hope in my dark places. The Bible says *"Write the vision; make it plain..."* Habakkuk 2:2

It was necessary to be clear about the visions in my heart and what I wanted in my professional life, my finances, my relationships, my body, my soul and my spirit. I created a vision board with everything I wanted to see happen in my life. Being clear on your vision is what will carry you through when you feel like quitting. So, I kept pushing!

Now it was time to invest in myself and to take care of me. Moms are nurturers by nature. We are wired to take care of our children and everybody else, most times to our own detriment. We put ourselves last on the list. Heck, I think sometimes we forget to put ourselves on the list. Single moms are notorious for this. I had to move myself to first on the list instead of last. Self-care is important to the process if you desire true success. I was getting nowhere fast by living that way and I knew I wouldn't be around in the long run if I continued. So one of the first things I did to invest in myself was hire a life coach, someone who could speak life into me and also hold me accountable. Next, I ate healthier and took nutritional supplements that would help me to get into better shape and feel better. Last, but one of the most important things I had to do was to forgive and trust God. By forgiving and letting go of all the hurt and pain, it allowed me to be free to move forward. It allowed God to reign in my life instead of allowing pain and rejection to rule me. I had to learn to trust God; He would speak and tell me, "You can trust Me! I am not like the men in your past, you can trust Me!" I didn't even realize that I hadn't trusted Him. My relationships with the men in my past were twisted and God had to remind me He was not like them. It was okay to trust Him; sometimes He still has to help me with this.

The Results

Go confidently in the direction of your dreams. Live the life you imagined. – Henry David Thoreau

Although I am still a work in progress, God has brought me so far. Sometimes it's necessary to go back to take inventory of what you used to be so you remain humble and thankful for the person you are becoming. I'm still working on myself daily, but also I am growing into the woman my destiny is calling for. I am in active pursuit of the dreams God placed in me. Each day I remind myself of the great things in store for me as I allow God to transform me from the inside out. I stated earlier that this was no longer about me… It's about you and anyone that may read this book. My story shared so your story can be told. All for God's glory!

Troyce Heath

First time author, Troyce Heath graduated with a Bachelors of Science in Economics with a concentration in Management Information Systems from Purdue University in West Lafayette, Indiana. She is certified through the Burton Morgan center for

Entrepreneurship and Innovation.

Her position as an IT consultant with an International IT Consultant Firm based in Paris, France requires much travel. The knowledge she has gained in her travels has inspired her to start her own IT consultant firm. It is her desire to participate in growing the family real estate business and creating a nonprofit organization to provide travel experiences to underprivileged children. Troyce is a certified 5D Coach and certified Human Behavior Consultant through Authentic Identity Institute. Together with her nonprofit organization, Troyce hopes to teach others how to be their authentic selves and give them the opportunity to see the world through different lenses. She plans to pay it forward as so many did for her throughout her teen years. Her favorite pastime is spending time with family, friends and her godchildren.

CHAPTER ELEVEN

The Making of a Prayer Warrior

In the beginning I did not know if God loved me. I thought that there must have been something in my life I had done to make Him upset, mad or even disgusted with me. At the age of 19 I realized that was not true. He loved me more than I could ever know or understand. In the midst of resigning my life over to God I went through it like no other. The spiritual warfare was real. Everything in my life seemed to be fair game; my health, my relationships, my finances, and the worst of them all - my spirit, all being attacked simultaneously.

God sent friends (angels if you ask me) to help guide me through. One particular young lady took it upon herself to guide and nurture me through the process to learn and understand that the growth and development of prayer was important to my life. We lived in the same dormitory and were close in age but she had more experience. She noticed and taught me the most valuable tool in her walk with God. She took me under her wing and made it clear she would not let me go. I soon went to her at all hours of the day for guidance and prayer. Before long I became dependent on and confident in her line of communication with Him. I was more confident in her ability to talk to Him and get results and not so much in learning how to pray like a warrior in the spirit. This was the beginning my heart contract with Him. Psalms 91 starts my journey to becoming a prayer warrior.

"He who dwells in the secret place of the Most High Shall abide under the shadow of the Almighty." Psalms 91:1

To dwell in the shelter of the Most High I had to get to that place. I had to get to a place where the things that use to control who I was and how I defined myself no longer could take precedence, He did. This took a lot for me. I soon realized that at my core I was a people pleaser. Everyone around me had to be happy. My desire was for them to experience the place I had been so blessed to experience so many times throughout my life. I had continued to ignore God because I thought there were two explanations of my happiness, luck or God. At the time I was dealing with better understanding that God did not hate me. He did not set out for me to be in pain and the pain experienced throughout my childhood was designed to strengthen who I was in Him and who He was in me, not to hurt or destroy me. Ultimately I would no longer fear aban-

> *To dwell in the shelter of the Most High I had to get to that place. I had to get to a place where the things that use to control who I was and how I defined myself no longer could take precedence, He did.*

120

donment; He was here with me and available. I had to decide and choose to dwell in the secret place He had created for me and Him.

I will say of the LORD, "He is my refuge and my fortress; My God, in Him I will trust." Surely He shall deliver you from the snare of the fowler And from the perilous pestilence. He shall cover you with His feathers, And under His wings you shall take refuge; His truth shall be your shield and buckler. Psalm 91:2-4

This is where my prayer life became real. It was no longer, "Dear Lord, thank you for this day. Thank you for my family. Thank you for a great opportunity to be educated at an international accredited university. Thank you for allowing me to have the funds to do all the things I want to do when I want to do them. Amen." My prayers became more like this, "Dear Father, forgive me for any and all things I have done today, yesterday and further in the past that are not of you. Forgive me for any moment I did not display love or who you are today. Forgive my family, friends and enemies for the same. Please bless my enemies, give them peace and clear-mindedness. Love on them Lord. Thank you for all and any trials and tribulations I did not understand about that my family has had to experience to become the amazing people they are. Please love on the ones who mock your name and refuse to believe you are real. Thank you for this amazing opportunity to receive an education to bless someone else's life. Please allow others to be blessed through my blessing and tribulations. Protect us and those who are in a place with questions about who You are. In Jesus name I pray, Amen."

"You shall not be afraid of the terror by night, Nor of the arrow that flies by day," Psalm 91:5

In the process of getting closer to God you soon realize that it is at night you are the most vulnerable. It makes sense. From the world's prospective it is harder to see at night. You are unaware of what is in the darkness until light is shed on it. This was true for me too in my growth with God. Everything from my past that had consumed my night had attempted to take over the new secret place that was set aside for me and Him. My guide taught me how to block all that out. I no longer was available via phone after a certain time. I had some of the most interesting attacks I had ever experienced; I learned how to not just pray through them but the importance of the night fight.

"Nor of the pestilence that walks in darkness, Nor of the destruction that lays waste at noonday. A thousand may fall at your side, And ten thousand at your right hand; But it shall not come near you." Psalm 91:6-7

In the mist of learning how to conquer my demons at night, I ran into the ones that crept into my daily life. I would spend many nights not getting any sleep at all because I was in the spirit and by day people would come from the woodworks! There were people I had never met that would tell me their trials and tribulations the first time we had an encounter. So I prayed; it was the first line of defense that my spiritual warrior had taught me, so I did. In the midst of these happenings I would get attacked on all sides. I would forget about a test or quiz or an assignment that was due that day. I cannot count how many times I had to go to my professors to ask forgiveness in honesty. I could no longer make excuses or fabricate the truth. In most instances they showed understanding in ways they normally stood against. This is where He showed me the numerous places of His grace and mercy.

"Only with your eyes shall you look, And see the reward of the wicked. Because thou hast made the LORD, which is my refuge, even the most High, thy habitation; No evil shall

befall you, Nor shall any plague come near your dwelling."
Psalm 91:8-10

When my prayer life changed, my focus changed. My relationship with God became my focus. I no longer wanted revenge or felt vengeance against those who had wronged me; I prayed for them. I became childlike in the spirit and accepted that being in His presence was the best place for me, my safe place and my refuge. The closer I got to Him the more serious the spiritual warfare became. I would come down with the flu or a stomach virus the day before a paper was due, three exams, an extra work shift and bible study all while watching others party the night before and ace the same exams. At first I would cry wolf like, "Why me Lord? Don't you see me trying to do this life thing your way, according to your will?" I saw it as a punishment. She would remind me that the attacks came with the charge of a prayer warrior. Life and death are in the power of the tongue and I was using mine to heal people and myself of the things that kept them and me in bondage.

"For He shall give His angels charge over you, To keep you in all your ways. In their hands they shall bear you up, Lest you dash your foot against a stone. You shall tread upon the lion and the cobra, The young lion and the serpent you shall trample underfoot." Psalm 91:11-13

God sent angels to protect me. I'm convinced that I probably only know about a tenth or less of the situations they shielded me from. Sit and think at every turn to guide and about had you gone on that trip where the plane crashed in flight, that party where everyone underage got locked up for drinking or had you not lost your keys before you left the house, that may have been you in that five-car pileup that no one survived. Yes, that is how it was for me too. I learned how to identify when I was under attack and surrounded myself with people able to do the same. This gave me the strength and ability to be less driven by my emotions in my faith and prayer and more warrior minded. I became less concerned with doing things my way. I cried out his name wherever and whenever the situation called for such and even when it did not. I spoke to everyone I met about Him; I wanted to be a display of His true love. I wanted those around me to have a genuine experience with Him.

"Because he has set his love upon Me, therefore I will deliver him; I will set him on high, because he has known My name. He shall call upon Me, and I will answer him; I will be with him in trouble; I will deliver him and honor him. With long life I will satisfy him, And show him My salvation." Psalm 91:14-16

This now brings us to the best part and by far the most unexpected part to me in the process of becoming a prayer warrior, His love! I thought I knew love before Him. My parents loved me; they clothed me, fed me and continued to sacrifice for me. My friends loved me; we went on trips together; they were my study partners; they were my shoulders to lean on. My pastors loved me; they were my Shepherds; they prayed for me; they exposed the truth in the word. There was (and still) is no comparison for the way which I did (and still do) experience His love. See, it is difficult to admit to those you care about that you have dark things going on or happening inside of you. I could (and still can) with Him. He exposed aspects of my character that threaten my ability to have a true relationship with Him. I no longer could hide the places of bitterness, anger, jealousy, pride or greed; He is the omnipresent. God always provided a remedy for each spiritual infection. Anger is by far the first and easiest emotion to display and feel but it covers up the true source, bitterness. Once this spiritual infection found its way into my life, it spread like wild fire. The medication was to deal with why I was bitter and what internal conflicts from my past were feeding the infection in my present. The charge was to forgive myself first for all those situations and then to forgive those whom in my mind took part in those places of pain. The same has been true for all spiritual infections that attempt to show their faces in my present life.

My journey with God in prayer has created its own identity of clarity. That there is a spiritual war is real and very apparent. If you have any doubt watch your local news and national news this evening; you will see the disasters that happened today alone. Becoming a prayer warrior has required that I put my doubts and any sign of lack of faith to the side to fight for the greater good, His people. They say the proof is in the pudding; well my prayer life is the pudding and God's continued grace, mercy and love are the proof.

Yalonda J. Brown

Yalonda J. Brown is a seasoned professional who has held corporate roles in the areas of executive management, sales, training, customer service and program management. Yalonda's drive and self-determination has resulted in a myriad of high functioning roles and professional accomplishments.

Mrs. Brown holds a Master of Science in Organizational Leadership and is a certified Development Dimensions International Facilitator. She has many philanthropic interests surrounding her passion for youth development and the empowerment of girls and women. Mrs. Brown is committed to improving the lives of all she touches through her efforts. Mrs. Brown is currently achieving this mission in her role as a Program Coordinator with the Center for Leadership Development, of which she is an Alumna. She is a member of the Board of Directors of AYS, Inc. as well as a member of the National Council of Negro Women.

Yalonda is an avid reader and has always enjoyed all forms of writing since she was a young girl. She also enjoys traveling, shopping, and has a creative spirit which she displays in her development of a line of greeting cards dedicated to breast cancer awareness and zeal for fashion.

Yalonda is on a mission to fully identify with her divine purpose. She desires to lead by example and fervently serve God in a way that He gets the glory in all things. She is a lifelong resident of Indianapolis, Indiana where she resides with her husband Vincent and twenty-year-old daughter, Kiara.

CHAPTER TWELVE

Bold, Beautiful, and Broken

"You are so smart."

"Your mother did not want you."

"You can do anything."

"You are too pretty to be broke."

"You think you are better than everybody."

"You lie like your Daddy."

"You are beautiful."

"God loves you."

These scripts have played in my mind at various moments throughout my life. Often I found myself confused, discouraged, and disheartened in my Christian walk. My confession of God as a child and church attendance throughout my teen years into adulthood made me seem ok. A prosperous life was my destiny, yet I lived spiritually poor. I walked and talked like a Princess but lived like a prostitute by allowing the exploitation of my time, energy, and pursuit of other worldly pleasures to slowly lure me away from God.

I lived "bold" with no regrets and no regard for consequences. Every accomplishment seemed to bring a disappointment. Each opportunity had a closed door. With gains, came setbacks; with love, came losses. It was never a doubt my destiny was a life filled with promise and purpose. I created some "beautiful" memories; yet I was "broken", inconsistent and prideful. I re-evaluated my values, character, and every relationship in my life.

For The Love of Money

1 Timothy 6:10 (NIV) *"For the love of money is a root of all kinds of evil. Some people eager for money, have wandered from the faith and pierced themselves with many griefs."*

It was the Christmas of my second grade school year when I realized that my maternal Grandparents had "money." I received everything I asked for that year, a Barbie Townhouse, my first Typewriter, Ms. Beasley Doll, and a room full of other toys and clothes. My Grandmother dressed me in custom made dresses with matching coats, Buster Brown shoes, and kept my hair done. She, without a doubt, loved her Lonnie; that was my family nickname. My Granddaddy only drove Cadillacs and would attend church every Sunday in his tailored suits. They were faithful in their church attendance and in their giving.

> *I created some "beautiful" memories; yet I was "broken", inconsistent and prideful. I re-evaluated my values, character, and every relationship in my life.*

My grandparents were both hard workers. Grandma worked traditional jobs while pursuing her degree in elementary education. In my younger years, I did not know what my Grandfather did for a living only that he left for work early each morning. Granddaddy was an entrepreneur and dependent on his "work day" results, he would come home and give me money. This became the ultimate pattern and expectation throughout my life.

As I grew older, I developed a hustle and grind mentality. I, also, developed a dysfunctional relationship with money. In a book titled, Mind Over Money, authors Brad Klontz and Ted Klotz, propose that "many of our money behaviors and dysfunctions resulted from 'money scripts', unconscious mental frameworks we develop to understand money."

As I worked and gained credit, I spent money as fast as I earned it. My Grandmother modeled healthy financial habits by maintaining a high credit score and putting money away in the bank or in the shoeboxes in the closet. Despite her attempts of teaching me financial stability, I did not like paying bills.

I faced my first eviction in college. I felt my grandparents would bail me out. For me, money represented a fix all, status, and security. Not once did I ever stop to consider it was not my money to begin with; it was God's. I was mismanaging His money and I paid for it well into my adulthood. Despite educational and professional achievements, I have spent the majority of my adulthood robbing Peter to pay Paul. This behavior resulted in me facing multiple bankruptcies, loss of my first home, and a myriad of avoidable stress, conflict, and ruined relationships.

For The Love of Motherhood

Proverbs 6:20-22 (NIV) *"My son keep your father's command and do not forsake your mother's teaching. Bind them always on your heart; fasten them always on your heart; fasten them around your neck. When you walk, they will guide you; when you sleep, they will watch over you; when you awake, they will speak to you."*

A mother's love.....well, it's complicated. Things were good until I disappointed my mother by getting pregnant at age sixteen and tried to cover it up. I believe this was the first time my mother called me out of my name. She put me out of the house and moved out-of-state. My grandparents came to the rescue. From that moment on, I carried a tainted view of unconditional love. There were multiple moments of reconciliation throughout the years yet we could not seem to get it right, leading to a lengthy estrangement. I continued to hurt and disappoint her and she continued to punish me with her silence. Though I so much wanted to please and prove to her I was fine through my accomplishments, the scripts continued to play in my mind of being told by hateful family members that my mother never wanted me anyway. It made it easier for me to dismiss the relationship.

Mother's Days, birthdays, holidays, etc., there was no interaction. Over the years, I had friends who had lost their mothers and/or I experienced the loss of their moms with them. I remember feeling so bad I could lose my mother without there being any real communication between us. Did the people in her life even know she had a daughter? Would I feel anything at all? When asked about my mother from people in my life, I would share the last major conflict as the reason for us not having a relationship. God sent adopted "mothers" to temporarily fill the gap who would remind me of the scripture, Exodus 20:12 (NIV) "Honor your father and your mother, so that you may live long in the land the Lord your God is giving you." I would dismiss it as if I had no accountability.

In the midst of all of this, I had become a mother to a beautiful daughter who is my pride and joy. My God! He chose me again! He gave a broken woman like me the honor of being a Mother. I planned my pregnancy but single motherhood was not in the long-term plan. I sought to give her the best possible life. We are close and even when I was pursuing careers and education, God covered us. Even when I was making decisions that could alter the trajectory of her life forever, God covered us.

My daughter was perfect; a good girl, smart, beautiful and God's unmerited blessing. I exposed her to a quality education, people and activities to help her grow. Reciting in song all 66 Books of the bible in pre-school, she loved going to church. Growing up, we were not a very affectionate family. There were few "I love you's" or open/public displays of affection attached to my memories. It was my determination to shower my daughter with love and affection. In her teen years, I remember asking her, "Why is it so hard for you to do what I ask?" "Why do you choose disobedience without regard for the consequences?" It was like looking into a mirror hearing the voices of my past. I had been no different.

Despite all the indicators of God's grace in my life, I could not say "no" to self and "yes" to God. My daughter, just like me, found it difficult to put my requests, interests, and needs above what she wanted, what she felt, what she desired. This is how I had handled God's commands and His plan for every part of my life including my relationship with my Mother. I had given up on thoughts of my mother sharing any milestones in my or her granddaughter's life. I repented and am thankful to say my mother and I reconciled six months before I married. We communicate regularly and our relationship is healing.

For The Love of "Man"

1 John 4:10(NIV) "This is love; not that we loved God, but that He loved us and sent His son as an atoning sacrifice for our sins."

Once I reached the dating age of sixteen, I entered my first 'real' relationship. From college on, I was never without a boyfriend and I was 'in love' with every one of them. I committed to each relationship; therefore, I did not consider myself promiscuous. After leaving my traditional college experience after three years, I continued to do life, grew in my career, and after some time and hard work, completed my education.

I was one who had meaningful females in my life who were my "ride or dies." It was not until I got older that I had girlfriend issues. After enduring a difficult breakup in my thirties, one of my girlfriends, who often gave me godly counsel, gave me a book about unhealthy soul ties. I realized I had unhealthy soul ties with female friends, men, and even with my career and money.

By this time, some of my close friends had married. There were a few times when I remember praying for a man who had a relationship with God, yet continued in ungodly relationships with men. Most of the male examples in my life were womanizers. My Daddy and Uncles were handsome and charming and women loved them. I identified with all their traits and saw them play out in my relationships.

My Granddaddy took care of home, but with that came a price. I remember asking my Grandmother why she put up with the other women and disrespect. I told her that would never be me. She told me in her gentle, sweet-spirited way that her faith was in God and she had invested too many years to leave. She told me if I did not get my mouth together, I would end up with no one. With the number of failed marriages and/or single women in my family, I decided I would never marry.

I was very opinionated. My Grandmother had me reading the newspaper since the age of five. She and my mother taught me to be an effective communicator. I had a vast vocabulary in "book" words and "street" words. Loyalty was a value I held high. If one broke the code, I was quick to tell them about it or dismiss them.

I gauged a man's purpose and staying power in my life by the three F's. A man interested in me had to fit into one of three categories: Fun, Finance, or "Fondle" (I used a different term back then.) Faith was not on my list of criterion. Though I was still seeking God's purpose for my life, I found the intimacy and "love" I was seeking in playing the role of Mistress. I do not share this to be boastful, but I had become comfortable in another form of dysfunction.

After many failed attempts to walk away, I made it a priority to understand my environment and the people and situations that were my sin triggers. There were people, places, and things that had to go as my priorities shifted. I desired a man that would care about my soul and salvation. I had been in an on-again/off-again relationship with the man that would become my husband. After we both stopped running away from God's plan for us, we both committed to seeking a relationship guided by godly principles. We stopped having sex (Oowee, this surpasses all accomplishments!), began premarital counseling before the initial engagement, and married a year and half later with my mother's blessing. 1 Cor 6:20 (NIV) *"you were bought with a price. Therefore, honor God with your bodies."*

As I bask in my newlywed bliss, I know God deserves all the glory and honor to bring me joy with a man who accepts all of me. In my husband, I have the three F's and much more…. including faith and intimacy with God who had already paid the ultimate cost for me.

For The Love of the Maker

"God uses broken things. It takes broken soil to produce a crop, broken clouds to give rain, broken grain to give bread, broken bread to give strength. It is the broken alabaster box that gives forth perfume. It is Peter, weeping bitterly, who returns to greater power than ever." Vance Harvey

I soon found myself in a season of pruning. In the world of gardening, pruning is the removal of parts of a plant, tree, or vine that are stifling growth, are no longer pleasing to the eye, or may be harmful to the health or development of the plant. In home gardening (e.g. rose culture), pruning enhances a plant's shape and flowering potential; new growth emerges.

I was certain my life was shifting when God used people, situations and breakthroughs to show me it resulted from nothing but His hands, grace and mercy. When I put my faith and dependency all in Him, He showed up and showed out in my life. Sometimes I would be in the midst of sinful acts and thoughts, a conviction would come over me to stop me dead in my tracks. I had countless encounters with receiving unsolicited counsel from people with no awareness of my circumstances. God knew!

My testimony is strengthened. I can now stand strong on what I know to be true. God stands on His promises and He was moving in my life. God is protecting me and my family. He is giving me great life experiences in the midst of the storms. His grace is allowing me to reach people and impact change through my professional accomplishments. Despite my challenges with my mother, He blessed me with two strong God-fearing

Grandmothers who took care of me in her absence. He is still sustaining me through the loss of my heart who had been my rock and main cheerleader since the age of 5, my maternal Grandma at the age of 92 in 2015.

Through the many trials and storms of my life, God was and is still pruning me. I am better prepared to grow and bloom so I may live and love abundantly.

To God be the Glory

1 Cor 10:31 (NIV) *"Whether, then you eat or drink or whatever you do, do all to the glory*

In my experiences as a daughter, friend, mother, co-worker, boss, and now wife, I believe all relationships are impacted because of actions related to six areas: communication, ego, humility, self-love, Christ-centeredness, and trust. I test every relationship in these areas to provide an accountability gauge for me and all involved. If there is a breakdown in any of these areas, the relationship suffers.

1 John 4:19-21 (NIV) reads, *"We cannot love God and at the same time turn away from our brothers and sisters."*

When I find it hard to love, I offer you a prayer I say often:

"Lord, help me to love others the way you love them. Jesus, you even loved those who hated, tortured, and killed you. You forgave them without hesitation. Help me to do that as well. Help me to let go of resentment or bitterness toward those in my life who have hurt me. Above all, take away any thought I may ever have of revenge. Help me to forgive and love my enemies. Only by the power of your Spirit will I be able to do that." Amen

Sometimes I sense God's presence in a real and powerful way through experiences with friends and family, praise and worship or through study. But then, there are those days in my life when peace seems so distant and praying is like pulling teeth; those days when nothing seems to go right and the difficulties are so overwhelming. I am here as a witness to the power of hanging in there. This is a grace thing. I am in a relationship with God and He loves me. The more I realize how much He loves me, the more I want to spend time with Him. I stopped making excuses and let go of the scripts that played in my mind that God would not restore my life in fullness because of my Christian maturity level, or I did not know enough about the bible, or the shames of my past.

God has placed in each of us everything we need to do the things we were put on the earth to do. God loves us unconditionally. Faith develops perseverance. To God be the glory, I am still a work in progress, being transformed from the inside out.

As a last note, I would like to share words adapted from the poem, **"When I Say I Am a Christian"** by Dr. Maya Angelou:

When I say ... "I am Broken"
I'm not shouting "I'm clean livin.'"
I'm whispering "I was lost,
Now I'm found and forgiven."

When I say ... "I am Broken"
I don't speak of this with pride.
I'm confessing that I stumble
and need Christ to be my guide.

When I say ... "I am Broken"
I'm not trying to be strong.
I'm professing that I'm weak
And need His strength to carry on.

When I say ... "I am Broken"
I'm not bragging of success.
I'm admitting I have failed
And need God to clean my mess.

When I say ... "I am Broken"
I'm not claiming to be perfect,
My flaws are far too visible
But, God believes I am worth it.

When I say ... "I am Broken"
I still feel the sting of pain.
I have my share of heartaches
So I call upon His name.

When I say ... "I am Broken"
I'm not holier than thou,
I'm just a simple sinner
Who received God's grace somehow.

Janice Batty-Prince

Ms. Janice discovered she had the gift of words and writing abilities as a young child. She started writing as an outlet for her feelings, which graduated to poetry. One of her teachers read her poems, "Wouldn't It Be Wonderful" and "Be Cool" and published them in the school's newspaper. Her first book, "Where Are The Intercessors? Somebody PLEASE Pray for Me!" was published and released in October 2013.

She has also written a series of youth bible study lessons entitled, "Wisdom For Your Youth." She desires to use her gift as a wordsmith to help others see their thoughts and ideas by putting words to their vision.

Though she loves to write and help others tell their story, she is passionate about her family, both immediate and extended. Her greatest joy is being in the kitchen preparing a meal for all to enjoy. When asked how it feels to be a published author, she responded, "I am simply a believer who is daily being transformed by the power of the Holy Spirit into the image of Christ, according to His Word in order to be put on display for His glory."

Ms. Janice was born in Gary, Indiana and graduated from West Side High School. As an entrepreneur, she is CEO of Excellence Administrative Office Solutions and Momma J's Brownies. She is the mother of six, grandmother of 19 and resides in Indianapolis, Indiana.

CHAPTER THIRTEEN

When Right Goes Wrong

It was May 14, 1999 when this letter arrived in my mailbox, very cordial and very well-written. I could tell right away the sender was very intellectual. After reading the letter, I put it on top of the computer and went on with my life. About three weeks later, I got this nudge from within to respond to the sender. I tried to shake it but couldn't. With no other recourse I flippantly said, "I don't even know where that letter is." Almost immediately that still small voice said, "It's behind the computer where you threw it." I don't remember throwing the letter back there but there it was, like it was waiting for me.

I sat down and reread the letter. I didn't know how to respond to this request for friendship. I sat at the computer and started to type. Much to my surprise, words just began to flow. As I typed I could feel the prompting of the Holy Spirit telling me what to say and what not to say. He chose my words and I typed them. Mission accomplished. The letter was complete and I mailed it.

I never expected a response to that letter or what pursued. We began to write weekly, then every few days. Letters turned into phone calls. Phone calls turned into visits.

During this time God was speaking. I remember sitting at work one evening listening to my headsets when I heard my name. I turned to see who was calling me but no one was there. I went back to work and heard it again. This time I knew who it was. I turned the music down and God began to speak to me right there at my desk. He said, "It's ok, let him get to know you. Allow him to see the real you. Give him the Book of Janice. He is the one that I sent." My mouth dropped open and tears began to run down my cheeks. A few days later I got the letter of letters from my new friend. It was 10 pages, typed! My new friend said that he had asked God if I was the one. He said God responded with, "She is the one you have prayed for." God told him he could trust his heart to me. Neither of us received these words with joyful hearts. There were too many negative variables. Kicking and screaming we decided to obey and entered into a relationship.

Against all odds, God refined and defined us. We grew in love from the inside out. Eight years, three months, three weeks and five days after that first letter, on September 1, 2007, we made a covenant before God and man to be husband and wife until death parted us. People still comment on how the presence of God was at our wedding and how His favor was upon our lives. I cannot deny any of it. We were the perfect couple in the sense that God had made us perfect in Him for each other.

My new husband, with his jaded past, landed a new career as an electrician trainee. Within three years he would be a licensed journeyman! The favor of God! I, with my broken past was hired by the school system. The favor of God! God put us in a three-bedroom home and within two months we had our first automobile. The favor of God! Our relationship was even sweeter. We were partners in every way. When we ministered together to family and friends, amazing things happened. Our home was a safe place where family and friends would come when they needed a peaceful place to escape the craziness in their life. Plus, my husband is an awesome teacher. I love the way he can expound the Word of God. He's a walking concordance. To say the least, I admired my husband.

Don't misunderstand me, I am not saying we always agreed or even that we always liked one another but at the end of the day, love always prevailed. God was elevating us in many ways. He was speaking Kingdom assignments over our life. We suffered no lack even with me only working nine months out the year. When we got married, I knew difficult times would come but I had no doubt we had what it took to overcome ANYTHING! I even believed I was prepared for the battle. I still say, you could not have paid me any sum of money to believe that we would go through what we went through and end up where we are now.

Two years into our marriage things started to change. My husband grew distant. We spent less time together. Money was coming up missing. Bank accounts were overdrawn and strange visitors were coming to our door. I pleaded with him to tell me what was going on. He said everything was going to be all right. I prayed. I cried. I spoke the word. Then he told me he was gambling. As soon as the words came out his mouth the Holy Spirit spoke to me and said he's using drugs. I was shocked and just looked at him and blurted out, "Are you doing drugs?" I remember he quickly said no and abruptly left the room. Things went downhill from there. We went to counseling but that was a joke. He charmed and lied his way through each session. I, on the other hand, looked like a raving maniac. This made me very angry. I grew bitter and vengeful. My husband's behavior escalated. His downward spiral was quick. Within six months, he had lost his career, spent all of our money, incurred immeasurable debt and had lost so much weight he looked like death warmed over. Through all this, God would not let me leave. I was his intercessor. I still loved my husband and was assigned to fight the spiritual battle that he couldn't.

I don't want to give the illusion that I was faultless or without sin during this time. I was not a willing participant in God's plan. I guess you can say I was reluctantly obedient, if there is such a thing. I was resentful; God and my husband knew it. I battled daily not to be bitter. I grew increasingly angry. I was hurt, disappointed, disillusioned, and disgusted. I felt betrayed. God was dealing with me. He was speaking to me giving me instruction, guiding me in the way I needed to go. This made me even more resentful. My heart was hurt. It was difficult to push past all that I was feeling. I was on an emotional roller coaster. With all that was going on inside me, I had to somehow still allow the love of God to flow through me to my husband. Sometimes obedience is HARD to say the least. IT WAS HARD!

How could something so right go so terribly wrong? During a sermon, I heard these words and I made them mine, "My anointing is stronger than this betrayal. My trust is not in man, my trust is in God…I forgive, I release and I let go so I can grow!" Much easier said than done, but nothing is impossible with God. Love never fails! In the strength of His grace, I was made able to obey.

After much external and internal struggle, my husband decided to enter a residential drug rehabilitation program. It was a twelve-month program with no contact for the first three months. I saw this as my way of escape. He left for the program on a Monday. By Friday I had gotten an apartment. Within three weeks, I had moved without him knowing where and was ready to start my life over again. My plan not God's; He intervened. He asked me not to leave His son with the promise of total restoration. He said He was calling me to a higher level of forgiveness. I did not understand what He meant. Then I heard these words, "True forgiveness, my kind of forgiveness, is when you can look at the person who wronged you and see who they are and not what they did." I had to put my wedding ring back on and go visit my husband. I remember before my first visit I gave God a list of demands. If this was His will, I had to hear and see certain things that day!

I arrived at the facility and they escorted me to the chapel where my husband was. When he looked up and saw me, I saw relief in his eyes. I saw hope. I saw something I hadn't seen in almost two years, his "for real" smile. In my predetermined plan, I had decided that it would not be easy for him to just step back into his God-given position of being my husband. I moved past him to my seat. Worship had begun and we were singing. He reached down and grabbed my hand (one of my demands). I immediately tried to get loose but he tightened his grip. I was not impressed (but my heart of hearts was)! Throughout the day, one by one, God systematically went down my list of demands. My husband had no clue what was going on. God was doing much needed work on my heart. On the drive back to Indianapolis, God began to speak to me. It was a long drive home full of tears and repentance. See, my list of demands were things I never thought would happen thus giving me every reason to end my marriage. God used my list to show me, first, His Sovereignty; second, He was still able to do exceedingly abundantly above all I could ask or think and lastly, my "god man," the man that I loved was still alive and worth fighting for. When right goes wrong it does not stop the plan of God, if we are willing to hear Him and obey.

It was a year of growth for both of us. It was a year of self-discovery. It was a year of healing and restoration. It was a year that should have been etched in our memory forever giving us the determination never to return to that place again.

SIN IS NOT WITHOUT CONSEQUENCE

God began the rebuilding process. During this process, my husband had to face a consequence of his actions and my heart had to embrace him, without looking back. God's grace was prevalent and His mercy once again overshadowed us. My husband came out of the fire of the consequence without even the smell of smoke. I came out with a love for him stronger than I had in the beginning. Though I was still working through some things, my heart was intact and I was determined to trust God to bring us through. It wasn't long before my husband was gainfully employed. Over the next two years we saw the amazing hand of God restore all that was previously lost. I learned that restoration does not necessarily mean you get back exactly what you lost. Expecting the same thing is so limiting. He restores you back to the original plan He has for you with endless possibilities. The methods/process may be different but the benefits of the plan are the same. It is all designed to bring you to HIS expected end. Sadly, some of us never reach that expected end. The dreaming stops. Moving forward stops. Stagnation sets in. A mere existence takes over what should be a vibrant abundant life. We get stuck and forget who and whose we are.

> *I learned that restoration does not necessarily mean you get back exactly what you lost. Expecting the same thing is so limiting. He restores you back to the original plan He has for you with endless possibilities.*

On the brink of stepping into all that God promised, the thief came to steal, kill and destroy. This time God allowed the choices made to run their full course. This time He did not intervene. This time He wanted us to choose Him. He wanted us to choose His plan. This time He wanted us to choose to let go of everything else and reach out to Him.

God gives us the power of free will. He will not override our will even when those choices lead us down the wrong path. There were roadblocks. There were warning signs. There were detour signs. But, for whatever reason, all ignored. Exercising his right of choice, my husband made a decision. He acted on that decision; I reacted to that decision and now we both have to live with the consequences of that decision. This time, we didn't recover.

On the heels of this, a few other rights went wrong. I lost my job; my church closed its doors and I lost my home. With all that God had spoken to me, I became sad. I withdrew into a world of sadness. I was grieving all that I seemed to have lost and what should have been. Sadness was killing me. Some may say I was depressed and afraid to move forward. They may be right. I do know it was never God's desire for my marriage to go through hell but it happened. My job, my church, my home...it happened. Things change and people change and not always for the better. Right went wrong! We make mistakes, wrong decisions, but it's not the end. Now I have a choice. I can trust God, reposition myself and choose to LIVE or I can allow the pain and uncertainty of the future to pull me out of my place of promise and live in sadness, depression, oppression, lack and fear. He's putting a demand on the gifts He has put in me. He is squeezing the oil of the anointing out of me. He is allowing my gifts to make room for me and bring me before great men (and women). Through my broken heart He is allowing me to pour into others. I don't understand it but I am no longer fighting it. Through the sadness and tears I must keep pressing. Through the brokenness of my heart I must keep pressing. It is through the pressing that my broken heart will mend. It is through the pressing that restoration of my soul and wholeness will come. It is through the pressing that God will be glorified. If I stop because right went wrong, I'll die. I can't die for God says LIVE! It's time for God to get the GLORY!

God is requiring me to move forward. It is a fast forward pace. Enough time has been wasted and I have to keep up. Do I feel like it? No! Do I like where I am? No! Are all the rights that went wrong in my life responsible for my present state? No! It is all on me!!!!! Another person's decision may have affected me but it carries no weight when it comes to me being true to me. It has no bearing on the responsibilities of my gifts and callings or the requirement to live on purpose to fulfill my destiny. Whatever the outcome, God has promised me no loss or lack. It is my responsibility to act on that promise. I must do my part. There is no escape or easy way out. With fear and trembling, I am learning to dream again. I am doing things I used to only imagine I would do. I am opening myself up to a life in purpose and I'm doing it on purpose.

I share this painful portion of my journey with you because I want you to see the light in your darkness. You may be in your darkest hour right now. You may be unhappy, confused, depressed and stressed. You may not know up from down. You may not have any answers, only questions. I get it. I live it every day. Every morning I have to pull myself out of bed and remind myself of what is in front of me. Every day I have to choose to not look back and dwell in the "what should have been." Some days I still cry. Today, it is only some days. A year ago it was every day.

Though I have no idea what your right is that has gone wrong, I have your way out. Don't hold on to the pain as a crutch; make it work for you. Let the pain become your driving force. Let the pain become the magnet that draws you into your destiny. Let the pain guide you to your passion. Let the pain fine-tune your spiritual ears to hear. Let the pain open your spiritual eyes to see. Hear and see God in the midst of the pain. Reposition yourself. Let go of the past. Press forward to be where you are supposed to be in life, where you want to be, doing the things you want to do. Yes, it's difficult but not impossible. It will take time and work but you will, we will recover.

I'll end with these encouraging words from Philippians 3:14-16:

"I'm not saying that I have this all together, that I have it made. But I am well on my way, reaching out for Christ, who has so wondrously reached out for me. Friends, don't get me wrong: By no means do I count myself an expert in all of this, but I've got my eye on the goal, where God is beckoning us onward – to Jesus. I'm off and running and I'm not turning back. So let's keep focused on that goal, those of us who want everything God has for us. If any of you have something else in mind, something less than total commitment, God will clear your blurred vision – you'll see it yet! Now that we're on the right track, let's stay on it."

We can do this, together!

PRAYER FOR THE AUTHORS
by Managing Editor, Coach T.

Father, I bring before you each author of this book collaboration. These are your daughters who you've set
on life's journey for kingdom purpose. They each have
unique stories and have come through challenges that
have greatly strengthened them. I thank you for the
call on their lives and their willingness to share their
stories to give you glory. You've touched their hearts
in a special way and for that I'm extremely grateful.
You've assigned angels as divine escorts leading and
guiding them along the path of righteousness daily.
They've now entered a new chapter of their lives by
releasing a portion of their stories to the world. I pray
your continued protection over their minds and emotions. Remind them daily of the people who are being
blessed by their faithfulness. Thank you for the healing and deliverance that comes as a result of the words
written on the pages of this book. I thank you that no
harm will come near their dwelling. I speak supernatu-
ral increase and elevation. Thank you even now for
allowing their gifts to make room for them. Open their
eyes to new opportunities and strategies to advance in
every area of their lives. I call their families, ministries
and future blessed. Your hand of favor is upon them.
Now cause fresh winds of your Holy Spirit to blow to
replenish, refresh and renew for their next leg of the
journey. Thank you for allowing their story to give
you glory. In Jesus' name. Amen

PRAYER FOR THE READER

Father I bring before you each reader of this book collaboration. I thank you for every word written that has pierced the heart and soul of each reader. I thank you for releasing your healing power through the testimonies shared. Thank you for cleansing tears and the joy of laughter. I ask now that you will give each reader 20/20 vision into the spirit real for correct insight and wisdom on how to move forward to give you glory with their story. Guide their thoughts and actions to align with your perfect will for their lives. I speak a release to propel them into their calling, purpose and destiny as they move forward in you. In Jesus' name. Amen

AUTHOR CONTACT INFO
(In Order of Appearance)

Tonya Kinchelow
"God's Grace is Truly Amazing"
Takinch@gmail.com

Carmen Randolph
"More Than A Conqueror"
CreateNoLimits@gmail.com

Carmencita Hughes
"Hallelujah Anyhow"
citahughes@gmail.com

Leslie Ann Wesley
"Abundant Life"
beinspiredbyleslie@gmail.com
www.beinspiredbyleslie.com

Tedria Denise
"The Pursuit of Radical Faith"
tedria.denise@gmail.com
www.tedriadenise.com

Deagria Cook
"I'm Still Standing"
deagria.cook@gmail.com

Nicole Emery
"The Training Ground"
NSEmery@gmail.com

Kennisha Cunningham
"Keep. Moving. Forward. Only Stop at Purpose Complete!"
KennishaCunningham@yahoo.com

Latonia Price
"My Shaking for the Greatest Glory"
effectiveliving.llc@gmail.com
www.effectiveliving-llc.com

Le Angela Hardiman
"Transformed"
Utransformed1@gmail.com

Troyce Heath
"The Making of a Prayer Warrior"
Heathtroyce2911@gmail.com

Yalonda J. Brown
"Bold, Beautiful, and Broken"
yalondajbrown@gmail.com

Janice Batty-Prince
"When Right Goes Wrong"
excellenceaos@yahoo.com

AUTHENTIC
IDENTITY
INSTITUTE

LIST OF SERVICES

COACHING
One on One & Group

KEYNOTE TALKS
Live Out Loud (ROAR)
SIGNificance
The Power of Authenticity

CERTIFICATIONS
5D Coaching Certification
Human Behavior Consultant Certification

SEMINARS
5D Authentically ME
5D Authentic Men
5D Authentic Identi-Teen
5D Authentically Me & You Couples Course
Authentically Me-Bully Free

ASSESSMENTS
(DISC) Personality Assessment
Spiritual Gift Assessment

JOHN MAXWELL CURRICULUM
Leadership Training
Mastermind Groups
Speaking

AIC BOOK PUBLISHING PARTNERSHIP DIVISION
www.authenticinstitute.com

Books Available
on Amazon or www.AuthenticInstitute.com

Hidden Identity

A Peace of Me

Made in the USA
San Bernardino, CA
22 June 2016